BY THE SAME AUTHOR

Rules of Warfare International Law Documentary Concerning Conflict (Shanghai Modern and Company)

Essay on China (Contributed to The Lawyers Chamber of India, in English)

Civilisation and Art of China (William Crosby & Son, London)

China Marvelled by Confucius (Thomas & Sons)

East and West (Hutchinson & Co., London)

Bartholomew was tutor to Tseng-Chee, Buddhist king, Fellow of University of Bengal, Indian Member of Parliament, General Arbitration Member of Court of Inquiry and Conciliation of the United Nations, has been Ambassador to the Court of the Queen as High and Permanent Courted International Justice, Special Commissioner of Chinese Government to the International Exhibition, in China, Author to Japan in 1934, Vice Ministry and Active Minister of Justice, Professor, Judge of Supreme Court, Peking, etc.

Barrister-at-Law, Honorary Bencher of Middle Temple, Fellow of University College, London, Member of Permanent Court of Arbitration, Member of Panel for Inquiry and Conciliation of the United Nations, Formerly, Ambassador to the Court of St. James's, Judge of Permanent Court of International Justice, Special Commissioner of Chinese Government for the International Exhibition of Chinese Art in London in 1935, Vice-Minister and Acting Minister of Justice, Nanking, Judge of Supreme Court, Peking, etc., etc.

Musings Of
A Chinese Gourmet

Food has its Place in Culture

By
F. T. Cheng
LL.D. (Lond.)

*Former Chinese Ambassador
to the Court of St. James's*

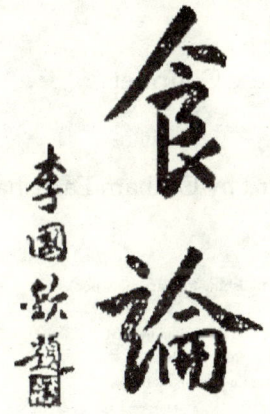

With a New Foreword by Graham Earnshaw

First published in 1954

Reprinted by
Earnshaw Books
Hong Kong 2008

Musings Of A Chinese Gourmet

By F. T. Cheng

With a new foreword by Graham Earnshaw

ISBN-13: 978-988-17326-0-6

© 2008 China Economic Review Publishing for Earnshaw Books

Musings Of A Chinese Gourmet was first published in 1954.
This edition with a new foreword is published by
China Economic Review Publishing for Earnshaw Books
Units C&D, 9/F Neich Tower,
128 Gloucester Road, Wanchai, Hong Kong

This book has been reset in 10.5pt Book Antigua. Spellings and punctuations
are left as in the original edition.

The Chinese character illustrations on many pages are all Chinese sayings
related to eating and drinking. They were not in the original, and are added in
this edition to add flavor to the mix.

"To the Ruler the people is Heaven;
to the people food is Heaven"

王以民为天 民以食为天

Kwan Tze

"No one does not eat and drink;
but few can appreciate (the nicety of) taste."

人莫不饮食也鲜能之味也

Confucius

TO
MY FRIEND
Mr. K. C. Li

Contents

Foreword by Graham Earnshaw   x

Preface   xv

I. Introduction   1

II. Is Cooking an Art or a Science?   12

III. What is a Good Cook?   17

IV. What is Good Cooking?   24

V. Importance of Good Cooking   31

VI. Schools of Cooking in China   40

VII. Classification of Dishes   50

VIII. Instances of Special Chinese Delicacies and Their Preparation   55

IX. Hints on Cooking   82

X. A Talk on Chinese Wine   106

XI. Dining as an Art   119

XII. A Discourse on Tea   136

Foreword
By Graham Earnshaw

THIS book was written at the end of an era—the half-way point of the 20th century when the communists occupied the whole of the China mainland, the Nationalists fled to Taiwan, and the curtain started to come down on a whole way of life— the urbane, bourgeois, sophisticated life of China's old elite. The communist leaders, led by Mao Tse-tung, were mostly peasants and they not only despised the effete culture of the old Mandarin class, they also saw it as a serious threat to their rule in the New China. They worked to destroy it, and in the Cultural Revolution of the mid-1960s, the culture of aristocratic old China was sniffed out entirely on the mainland.

It was a shame, because while there was corruption, arrogance, waste, decadence and sloth in the world of the Mandarins of old China and their successors, the Nationalist elite of the early 20th century in their Western suits and cheongsams, there was also much of value, including a food and alcohol culture that over centuries and even thousands of years had been refined to the most extraordinary detail.

That culture survived in a form in Taiwan and to some extent in Hong Kong through the decades that followed the communist takeover, but the mainland was for many long years reduced to bowls of rice and noodles and little else. In 1978, when I came to the mainland, the streets of even the largest cities were almost as dark as a tomb, and the number of restaurants in Shanghai and Beijing could be counted on one hand. It is almost unbelievable to remember it when looking at the neon-lit multi-level food palaces that now abound in all China's cities.

F.T. Cheng, the author of this book, was definitely a member of that old Chinese elite whose world was shattered by the communist victory. At the moment when the world ended, in 1949, he was the Chinese ambassador to the Court of St. James, in other words, to the United Kingdom in London. He dined occasionally with Princess Elizabeth, soon to be queen, and her husband Prince Philip. He was an intellectual who spoke English with the same old world charm as he no doubt did Chinese. And once things stabilized in the early 1950s — with Britain at that point still recognizing the government in Taipei as the rightful government of all China — he decided to write his "musings" on the theme of Chinese food and drink.

He published this book in 1954, and incredibly there is absolutely no mention of the recent spot of trouble that had barred him from ever returning to mainland China. He had anyway spent more than two decades living in London and New York, and he would probably have been somewhat unhappy to be thrown back into the messiness of the reality of Chinese life.

Mr Cheng was certainly a gourmet, and this book is a collection of what would no doubt have been long and entertaining dinnertime monologues as his guests sat at a round table in his residence or at one of the best Chinese restaurants in London and New York, and listened to his articulate, learned dissertations on such topics as how to prepare shark's fin soup, how to brew the perfect cup of Chinese tea, and how to judge a good Chinese rice wine.

Of course, the food, the tea, the drinks would all have been prepared and delivered by an army of cooks, maids and servants who hover in the shadows of this delightful work.

Mr Cheng—it would be impolite and inappropriate not to address him as Mr at all references—was Cantonese and a great fan of that great southern school of Chinese cooking. He gives precise recipes for many of the key dishes, and very detailed directions on how to prepare them. These recipes have a value, and people who know about Chinese cooking will enjoy comparing the recipes and preparation approach of Chinese cuisine in the early decades of the 20th century. But of even greater value, I think, are his musings on life and the Chinese character that spring out of his gourmet mental ramblings.

He quotes liberally from, or rather sprinkles his text generously with, quotations from the Chinese classics and from the literature of England. Shakespeare, Bacon (how apt), and Milton are all referred to along with many others. Mr Cheng, who also quotes from his own poems, is clearly at pains to demonstrate to the fullest that he is more educated in English than all but a small number of Englishmen, the aim being not only to show off, but also to establish his credentials for pontificating at such length about the culture of China.

Food, says Mr Cheng, is not just a necessary activity to stay alive, it should also be an integral part of culture. Chinese cooking is both a science and an art. Unlike most books which point to China having invented paper and gunpowder, he talks instead of how China invented soy sauce. He explores the regional schools—Sichuan, Canton, Shanghai, Beijing and beyond. He tells anecdotes which are charming and sometimes dismissive of the fairer sex. He waxes lyrical on tea preparation and the table games that accompany wine drinking after the food has been cleared away by the butler and his staff.

We can be reasonably sure he would not have been impressed by today's Chinese supermarkets, with their shrink-wrapped chicken feet, pre-cooked dumplings and surly assistants. He talks with Confucian approval of how, in his day, "[a] shop assistant or cook performs his duties cheerfully with a high sense of dignity and equality".

The alcohol culture of China is something that is particularly of interest to me, not because I am heavy drinker—I am not—but because it really does seem to reflect the depth and cultural significance that Mr Cheng ascribes to the whole Chinese process of ingesting matter.

In Western drinking, the drinkers may clink glasses at the start of the session and say "cheers". But after that, they basically all drink alone, taking a sip or a gulp of the liquid whenever the fancy takes them and with no regard to what other members of the group are doing.

At a traditional Chinese banquet, this would far surpass rudeness to be unthinkable. At such a banquet at a round table, there is a small glass in front of each guest, minded by young ladies who hover in the background, watching consumption with the eyes of a hawk (pre-roasted), and moving with the speed of a civet cat (pre-braised) to instantly replenish all empty glasses to the brim.

None of the guests picks up a glass and drinks alone. Absolutely every time a glass is raised, it is to toast someone else around the table—a glance at the other person, a few words (or not), a quick draining by both of the shot glasses followed by a raising of the glasses again to show that they are empty. Then the conversation continues, and all parties watch for the next opportunity to propose a toast. It is all about social manipulation, the manipulation of relationships, and in terms of cultural sophistication, it is beyond anything possessed by the West.

Of course, the aim is also to consume large amounts of alcohol and get thoroughly soused. But it is done in a way that is redolent of another era and culture, far, far away from Western fast food and a round of drinks at the corner pub. And it survives still in provincial China, although less and less in the coastal cities.

That is a long sidetrack. But what I mean to say is that I agree with Mr Cheng. There is much that is true in his Musings. Food and drink are an integral part of Chinese culture and reflect its richness and depth.

He wrote this book all those years ago to educate Westerners about his homeland, to show them that there was more to Chinese food culture than chop suey. But Chinese people of the 21st century could perhaps learn and benefit even more from spending a little time with Mr Cheng as he launches into another monologue on preserved duck's eggs, beansprouts or the distinctions of Fukien cuisine.

Graham Earnshaw
Shanghai
April 2008

The Chinese character illustrations on many pages are all Chinese sayings related to eating and drinking. They were not in the original, and are added in this edition to add flavor to the mix.

Preface

IT MAY seem strange to some of my readers that a man after having been judge of the "World Court" and Ambassador to the Court of St. James's, apart from having held other offices, should on the eve of his seventieth anniversary think fit to write a book on what largely has to do with food and living. But my friend Dr. Chung Yu Wang, engineer, scientist, and philosopher, with a number of standard words to his credit, and, above all, well-known gourmet in the true sense of the word, thinks otherwise. He urged me to write such a book as long as thirty-odd years ago, when we both attended the Washington Conference, and has since quoted me as "*Maître*" in his articles on cooking or food. Before I surrendered to his persuasion he said, as a *coup de main*, "It is exactly because you have been this and that and have reached your present age that you are most qualified to take up this task and should leave a bit of your 'wisdom to posterity'. Don't you know Brillat-Savarin's well-known remark that 'the discovery of a new dish does more for the happiness of mankind than the discovery of a new star'? Don't you know, as you must, that dinners have become the means of government and diplomacy, and that the fate of nations is often decided at a banquet? Historically speaking, no great event ever happened without its being previously planned or determined at an elaborate meal. Thus, you see, the writing of such a book is but the continuation of your previous functions in a different form. Knowing the world as I do, I even venture to think that you will be remembered more by the contribution you will have made through the book that I now urge you to write than by the services you have rendered through the performance of your official duties, meritorious though they are."

These are big words, indeed. All I wish to say is, since one must live, one must eat, and since one must eat, one may just as well eat well, and, in order to eat well, one must know or learn to know good cooking, which is a contribution to the pleasures of life, in general, even more important than that of music, fine arts, and literature; for, if necessary, one can dispense with the latter but not with food. Indeed, a nation that produces good food will also produce good music, good painting, and good literature; for all these form integral parts of what is known as *culture*, of which food is an important factor. It is no less than an English Nobel Prizeman, T. S. Eliot, who says:

"If we take culture seriously, we see that a people does not merely have enough food to eat but a proper and particular *cuisine*: one symptom of the decline of culture in Britain is indifference to the art of preparing food. Culture may even be described simply as that which makes life worth living."[1]

From the national point of view good cooking contributes to national economy and national health; for good cooking does not waste and, as it makes the daily meal an enjoyment, must have a beneficial effect on the soul and body of the people, unless affected by poverty or abuses.

My friend has not only urged me to write this book but also

---

1. *Definition of Culture*, p. 26.

furnished me with an abundance of ideas. It is he who suggested the main title of the book but I am responsible for
the sub-title. To profess myself to be a gourmet would be
presumptuous. If any justification for the appearance of this
book is needed, the words of a poet may be quoted: *"We may
live without books, but a civilized man cannot live without cooks."*
Personally, as it was written during a short re-visit to America after thirty years, the work done has also been a pleasant
pastime.

New York
1954

CHAPTER ONE

Introduction

IN THE development of her civilization and institutions China all along, until comparatively recent years, followed her own way and her own ideas, whether in religion, philosophy, art, literature, law, conventions, or in government. As a result, everything Chinese, with all its perfection or imperfection, bears the distinctive "hallmark" of the Chinese people, who thus gradually built up what is known as Chinese culture or the Chinese way of life. While China has developed her civilization and culture entirely by her own effort and in her own way, some nations in the East owe theirs partly, if not wholly, to hers. Though the Chinese were ruled by the Mongols in the *Yuan* dynasty (A.D. 1277-1368) and by the Manchus in the *Ching* dynasty (A.D. 1644-1912), these conquerors were absorbed by the Chinese.

All this is widely known and well recognized by the world. What is not known or recognized is that all this has something to do with her food, which is just as distinct and unique in nature as her art, philosophy, and literature, and without which her artists, philosophers, and poets might not, perhaps, have so flourished. It is her food that stirs the imagination of her thinkers, sharpens the wits of her scholars, enhances the talents of those who work by the hand, and enlivens the spirit of the people. Thus it has helped to create a nation peace-loving, contented, patient, persevering, cheerful, and philosophically minded; because in it the Chinese find something that makes life worth living. Nay, if you ask why the Chinese have the largest population of the world, the answer is, "Their food!"; because, since it has helped to create a nation with such characteristics as just described, it is only logical that it must have, at least indirectly, contributed to the latter's reproduction. If you ask why the Chinese, and particularly their womenfolk, always look younger than their age, the answer is the same: because, as every dish, if well prepared, is a delicacy, it tends to harmonize the natural growth of the body. It is no less an authority than Brillat-Savarin who says:

"A series of strictly exact observations has demonstrated that a succulent, delicate, and choice diet delays for a long time and keeps aloof the external appearances of old age. It gives more brilliancy to the eye, more freshness to the skin, more support to the muscles; and as it is certain in physiology that it is the depression of the muscles that causes wrinkles, these formidable enemies of beauty (to which may be added 'flabbiness' and 'fleshiness'), it is equally true that, all things being equal, those who know how to eat are comparatively ten years younger than those ignorant of that science."[1]

The reason is simple. If, for instance, you feed every day on a large piece of meat like a pre-war steak, the spirit of the animal will creep behind you and whisper: "Monsieur" or "Madame", as the case may be, "I am much honoured by your fondness of my flesh. May you have very good health and your body develop like mine!"

A disciple of Confucius once observed that "by hearing the music of a country one may know (something of) the charac-

---

1. *Physiology of Taste*, p.115.

ter[1] of its (ruler)". There is much truth in this, for in ancient times the ruler was absolute, whose taste, good or bad, would be reflected in everything national and certainly in music, which ancient China regarded as a means conducive to harmony, public orders, and good morals. In modern days one may say that the National Anthem of a country, unless falsely or badly composed, may furnish some guide to the character of its people and its national aims. If this is so, the food of a nation must be some guide to its culture. It reflects the taste of the people, and, if it is good, shows their good sense in choosing the materials, their genius in inventing it, their talents and patience in preparing it, and, above all, their knowledge of how to make life enjoyable. Therefore, one may well say: "Tell me what the food of a people is and I will tell you what their culture is like."

In this light, if you ask which part of New York is most cultured, the answer is, "China Town"! Why? Because of the delicious food you can find there. Apart from such special delicacies as Shark's fin, "Bird's nest", "Dragon" fish skin, Bear's paw, Duck's tongues, Duck's or goose's feet, Fish lips, Fish gill, Turtle's skirt, Bamboo shoot, Lotus root, Lotus seeds, Bean sprouts, Bean curd, Abalone, delicious fungus of various kinds, and many others, all of which are

---

1. Lit., "Virtue"; but it cannot mean virtue alone. It must have included vice too; therefore "character" is the correct rendering.

[3]

even undreamt of in other cuisines, you will find that everything you eat there, whether it is meat, poultry, sea food, vegetable, or dainty refreshments, is a delicacy, because of its infinite varieties of way of preparation and the delicate flavour it embodies. People go there not simply for satisfying their hunger but principally for gratifying their taste. What a pleasure the art of cooking can offer to life! And what better evidence can there be than for a nation being excellent in this form of art as a testimony of high culture? A nation, though uncultured, may, all of a sudden or at times, produce a genius, whether in art or in literature, but only a people of culture can have a good cuisine; because the former is particular and transient, whereas the latter is general and permanent. The one, at most, shows that the race concerned is capable of being cultured and even great; the other proves that the people have already cultivated their taste and the art of living to such an extent that they must have reached a high standard of culture, without which the possession of such a heritage as good cuisine is impossible; for it reflects their way of living and is common to all.

Food is not the only mark of culture in New York's China Town. There, the average working man, whether a shop assistant or cook, performs his duties cheerfully with a high sense of dignity and equality; men address one another as brothers, women as sisters; if they happen to be elderly, they are addressed as uncles or aunts, as the case may be. You will never hear a "salutation" begun with "I say!" If you enter a shop or restaurant at the same time as others, though strangers, those who are younger than you will, in nine cases out of ten, concede you precedence by allowing you to enter first. If you by chance meet at a restaurant a younger man known to you, he will, on leaving, more often than not, come to your table and bow to you, saying "good-bye", prefaced with a few words of salutation. A waiter thanking you for your tip would say "*Hsing Wei*", meaning in Cantonese "your gracious gift". At leisure hours you can always find some elderly persons to talk with you, over a pot of tea, on high ethics, such as benevolence, righteousness, propriety or moral rules of conduct, wisdom, and sincerity; provided, perhaps, you introduce the subject with words like "Times are changing now!" Such a talk with a stranger at a chance meeting would be inconceivable elsewhere, but in China Town it is quite in order. Sometimes at a restaurant one may hear said that So and So are dining "feet to feet" — meaning playfully an affectionate couple, young or old, dining happily together by themselves — an expression far more graphic and graceful than "*tête-à-tête*". If a member of the fair sex should give one a glad eye, this would be called "A twist of the autumn wave"! How poetic! And you can hear such a language only in China Town. People there may have radios but they would not turn them on to listen to songs like "I LOVE YOU, I love you . . ." They would rather, for that matter, turn on the gramophone and listen to such songs as the *Pi Par*:

"At thirteen I'd the *Pi Par* learned to play.
Within the realm of art I was the queen,
Enthroned by masters of no mean display.
My charm stirred every jealous woman's spleen.

Rich youth competed hard to win my love;
Each piece I played won for me priceless gifts;
Jewels of divers kinds I had enough;
Wine often stained my purple skirts and shifts.

Year by year I had the days enjoyed;
Past Springs and Autumns raised no dread alarms;
Began to fade my beauty unalloyed;
My mother died; my brother flew to arms!

Broughams and horses honoured less my door;
A merchant I espoused, when I was old;
But it is gold and silver he loves more;
The pain of parting on him has no hold."[1]

"Way of living" is quite a different thing from standard of living and still more from "way of life". The latter is bound up with the entire culture of a people and their traditions, reflecting the general conduct of the people as a whole; it has little to do with living and still less with food. When a person says: "We have our way", he refers to the "way of life" of the people he represents; when one speaks of "way of living" or "standard of living", he refers to the living conditions of a people. But though both concern living, they differ widely: the one reflects the culture and wisdom of the people, the other their economic means and resources. The standard of living of a nation may be low, owing to general poverty due to undevelopment of resources or lack of scientific knowledge to make labour productive, or to other causes such as war or natural disasters; yet its way of living may be wiser and yield more pleasure than that of a people whose standard of living is higher, which, in the way of food, often means only eating more, wasting more, and costing more, but not living better. For instance, the standard of living of the average Frenchman may be low in comparison with the richer nations. Yet every dish of note in a fashionable Western restaurant outside

---

1. See full poem in *East and West* by the same author, pp. 52-3 (Hutchinson & Co.).

France bears a French name, and a meal at a French home, however humble, enables one to learn a great deal as to how a very common thing can be made into something very enjoyable. In this respect, the Chinese have even more to offer, if not to teach. Incidentally, living must be distinguished from life. It is thus possible that a people may have a high standard of living (that is, plenty of food and other material things), because it has the means, and yet very little life (i.e. joy derived from material things), because it lacks the knowledge or culture to make life enjoyable in spite of the means it possesses.

Thanks to the wisdom of their sages, the Chinese as a people have been taught since ages past to find enjoyment of life and be happy even in the meanest circumstances. "Even if I (am so poor, as to have to) use my bended arm (to serve) as my pillow," says Confucius, "I can still be happy".[1] Thus the Chinese have learned at a very early stage of their civilization that true happiness and enjoyment of life do not depend entirely on material things; that even the commonest things, whether in the form of art or in the form of food, can be turned into something that will afford pleasures to life, and that taste, and not the desire for things rare or difficult to obtain, should be cultivated, so as to make the means of enjoyment of life accessible to all. As a result, the

1. *Confucius: Lun Yu*, Pt. VII, Ch. 15.

Chinese in general, and particularly their country folk, have, by training or association, acquired the habit of being able to find enjoyment in many simple ways, such as celebrating a festival, listening to a fairy tale, sipping, in company with friends, a cup of tea—nay, even gazing at the moon or the Milky Way, as if they could see "tongues in trees, books in the running brooks". Above all, they are able to control that restlessness of spirit often apparent among people of the West and to adapt themselves to circumstances without feeling undue strain from the change. In late years one often hears spoken, or reads in books or journals, the grand phrase "freedom from want", as one of the aims of constructing a better and happier world. The word "want" means, of course, the need or lack of those essential material things principally required for keeping a person from hunger and cold and for affording him a reasonable amount of comfort. This noble aim is certainly fundamental and, unless it is achieved, the hope for a better world would be futile. In this connection, it is remarkable that the Chinese have for centuries been taught by their philosophers, as a means of attaining happiness, to learn and try to be "free from 'WANT' ". This "WANT" means an ardent desire for things that can be dispensed with as a condition to the enjoyment of life and true happiness. In other words, in order to be able to enjoy life one must not become "slave" to things, just as one must not become an addict to certain things. "If things that are difficult to obtain are not prized," says Lao Tze,[1] "people will not steal; if what is desirable is not seen, the mind will not be disturbed. No fault (as a cause of calamity) is greater than being passionate for possession."

With such an outlook of life, and realizing that food is a dai-

---

1. Founder of Taoism, whose exact date of birth is controversial but who is often considered as a contemporary of Confucius.

ly necessity and dining a daily performance, the Chinese exert themselves to make food a source of enjoyment. One often sees in streets in China, or even in Hong Kong and Malaya, what are known as "street kitchens", to which a labourer, after his day's toil, will resort with a choice piece of meat, instructing the cook, on the spot, to cook it to his own liking. If even a workman is so particular about his food, the taste of the people in general can be imagined. It is this general interest in good living that the Chinese, thanks to their genius, have, through centuries of experience and experiment, developed what is known as the Chinese cuisine. They do not depend on rare materials to make their food palatable: they depend on method and skill. Thus rice and wheat, though very common food forming, in fact, the main diet of the people, are at a small cost made into delicacies in scores of forms, notably the great varieties of noodles and meat packets, called *Chao Tze*, both of which were probably introduced into Italy by Marco Polo, and afterwards developed into *Spaghetti* and *Ravioli* respectively. But if you taste the originals you will see the vast difference between them and their "naturalized descendants". Though tardily and somewhat reluctantly, the world has gradually begun to take notice of Chinese food. In almost every restaurant of note in New York City, for instance, what is called *Chow Mein*, i.e. noodles cooked in a certain way, figures in its menu. All over the world

there are Chinese restaurants; many of them cater mostly for non-Chinese. In New York alone they number several hundreds if not yet a thousand. I often think that these restaurants are not merely places for Chinese food but are really invisible vehicles of Chinese culture.

Nevertheless, most Westerners, except Continental people and those who have tasted Chinese delicacies in the East or in a place like China Town in New York or San Francisco, think that the best dish the Chinese cuisine can offer is what is known as "Chop Suey", which, though it can be very tasty and appetizing, is far from being a Chinese delicacy and is hardly known as such in China. It is only a made-up dish specially prepared for American customers by pioneer Chinese restaurants early set up in the United States. It consists of slices of several kinds of vegetables, such as bamboo shoot, mushroom, onion, bean sprouts, celery, cabbage, tomato, and water chestnut, cooked together with fillets of meat or chicken, as will be described in a later chapter. However, it is so popular in America and England that some Chinese restaurants in these countries sell nothing but "Chop Suey".

In connection with this dish there is a story which may now be told. The late Mr. Ernest Bevin, former British Foreign Secretary, dined several times at the Chinese Embassy and, every time, was given, partly, Chinese food. One evening he was asked whether he had ever had Chinese food before, and he answered "yes", adding that he often went to Chinese restaurants before he took office. Hearing this I naturally asked him what dish he liked best and his answer was, "No. 8."[1] This sounded like a conundrum. Therefore I followed up my

---

1. For the convenience of non-Chinese customers dishes in Chinese restaurants dishes are often designated by numbers, so that they may be ordered without the inconvenience of pronouncing Chinese names.

question with a series of queries like "Animal? Mineral? Vegetable?" In other words, I asked him whether it was meat, poultry, or sea food, and his replies were a successive "No." Then I said, "I know it now!" He dined at the Embassy a few weeks later and "No. 8" prominently figured in the menu. After he had tasted it, I asked him whether it was right, and his answer was "Quite right, but you have improved it!" This was, in fact, "Chop Suey". As "No. 8" became so well known afterwards as a gastronomic choice of the Foreign Secretary, it always formed an item of the menu in subsequent "diplomatic" dinners during my term of office, even on the occasion when their Royal Highnesses, Princess Elizabeth (now Her Majesty the Queen) and the Duke of Edinburgh, honoured us with their presence at an informal dinner in April 1949.

To conclude, it may be observed that culture has nothing to do with motor, radiator, refrigerator, elevator, or waste, but something to do with eating, drinking, cooking, living, and taste.

CHAPTER TWO

Is Cooking an Art or a Science?

THIS question is often asked but will, perhaps, never receive a perfect, simple answer. Roughly speaking, one may call it a combination of both; that is, so far as the means of cooking are concerned it is a science, and, so far as the application of the means is concerned, it is an art, though the preponderance is inclined to the latter. The same applies in various degrees to medicine, law, and other professions, taking cooking as a profession. For instance, we do say "medical science" but we speak of "the art of healing". Similarly, though we say "the science of law", everybody knows that cross-examination of witnesses and, indeed, the very practice of law itself are an art. It is, I believe, the same with other professions *mutatis mutandis*. To realize this at the outset is important. For though what may be regarded as belonging to the sphere of science can be mastered, such as learning by heart the details of a recipe, what comes within the province of art can never be properly executed without intelligence, patience, experiment, and experience. A man may have "mastered" the rules of swimming from books, but if he plunges into the sea the first time merely equipped with a book knowledge, however profound it may be, the chances are that he will be drowned. The same may happen to one who first attempts to cook, but the result would not of course be so disastrous, though he may get a few burns, if he is not careful, and will probably make a mess of the stove. However, one must not be discouraged by his first experience to think that he can never be a good cook, like the young lawyer who, having lost his maiden case badly, became so dispirited that he closed his chambers and went in for another profession. There are born-cooks, just as there are born-poets and born-painters; but the average cook has become such merely through necessity, practice, experience, and in some cases, like the professional class, training, just as one who has to learn the three R's. Indeed, ever since fire was discovered, the thought of cooking has dawned on the mind of man, and as soon as cooking was discovered, human beings began to devise means to make their food appetizing and tasty. Therefore it is true to say that every man has the instinct to cook, though it may lie dormant in him and he may be unconscious of it either through circumstances or through inertia. Put a man or woman on an isle, from which he or she has no means of escape, but on which every utensil for cooking and all ingredients for good food are provided, and you will see that after a year or two he or she will turn out to be at least a fairly good cook. I often think that if Napoleon, when confined on St. Helena, had been left to do his own cooking, he would certainly have emerged to be a wonderful cook and, with his genius, contributed to the world some marvellous dishes, doing perhaps, greater honour to his memory than all his military campaigns and his Civil Code (*Code Napoleon*), of which he was so proud and which he him-

self said would last longest in the memory of posterity.

This simple truth has been eloquently demonstrated by the many Chinese ladies who live in New York. For various reasons, they have to do the daily cooking themselves, though most of them have never before in their lives done more in this line than boiling water for making tea. Thanks to this necessity which is the mother of invention, some of them have thus come to be able to produce some very good Chinese dishes fit for a prince or millionaire, or rather the most consummate gourmet; for men of standing or of wealth do not necessarily have a good taste, though they have ample opportunities of tasting good food.

To the Chinese cooking is entirely an art; not that Chinese cooking has no scientific basis, but because Chinese cooking involves, in general, a complicated process and is of an infinite variety, while Chinese cooks derive their knowledge more from experience than from books and trust to the hand, the eye, the nose, the tongue, and often the ear as well, rather than depend on the scale or the watch. In boiling eggs the Western method of counting by the minutes is certainly more scientific and more reliable; but in other cookery, even in the simple case of cooking rice, one has to trust to one's senses rather than to the watch.

In China there has always been, and, I believe, in other countries too where the culinary art is prized, such as France, there can be, to various extents, a distinction between what may be called "dishes by the gourmet" (士大夫食家菜) and "dishes by the professional cook" (廚子菜). The former, though they are the work of the amateur and may not always maintain a uniform standard (just as the masterpieces of an artist are not necessarily always of the same excellence), invariably bear the evidence of thoughts, ideas, skill, and attention and, above all, present at their best a taste so exquisite and so unique that it is beyond the imagination of the ordinary professional man. In fact, it is through this channel that many famous Chinese dishes, in vogue at the present day, have been created; for Chinese scholars are always proud of being gourmets, just as Alexandre Dumas *père* was proud that his cookery had never received any adverse criticism, though many people found fault with his books,[1] and it was to them that many famous cooks of the past owed the perfection of their art.

At least so far as Chinese cooking is concerned, because it is largely a work of art, it may be said that the man of taste, the gourmet, has played a greater part in the development of good cooking than the person called cook; for the latter is in general merely one who is able to prepare a meal of some sort, whereas the former, though he may not have done more cooking himself in his life than boiling an egg, knows what is good or bad, and it is this knowledge, when imparted to the cook, that leads to the improvement of cooking. In this light, criticisms by a person knowing nothing about cooking but a great deal of what is agreeable to the palate are not only legitimate but a source of contribution to the art of the cuisine; for cooking and tasting are two functions, separate and distinct, just as one may well criticize the shape of a table or the

饮食起居

1. *The Prodigal Father*, by Edith Saunders (1951), p. 171.

setting of a picture without oneself being a carpenter or painter. It follows, therefore, that a cook may even be "trained" or "polished" by one who knows how to eat but not how to cook; provided the cook can be made to realize that the art of cooking consists not merely in having something cooked in some commonly accepted ways, but in thus producing or creating what is pleasing to the palates of others—particularly those who can appreciate good cooking—and that their opinions should not be frowned upon as those of "armchair" critics. Such realization presupposes good temper, patience, and a willingness to improve. The lack of any of these "virtues" would make "training" or "polishing" impossible. Worse would it be if he were imbued with an excessive conviction of what he is able to do, or over-self-confidence, which may be a form of "courage" and, in that sense, a "virtue", but is fatal in art—no less in the art of cooking. To do him justice, he may, in certain dishes, have good reasons for his own way, but these may have only a "regional" taste, as will be discussed in a later chapter: for instance, those that are excessively flavoured with different kinds of sauce, having a dominant taste of their own. If he abides by his conviction, he cannot be reformed.

By way of conclusion, without pretending to be a gourmet, but thanks to the enlightened comments of these connoisseurs of food or men of taste who at different times honoured my table with their company, I was able to "train" two cooks—one in Peking, who afterwards was much sought after as cook; the other in Nanking, who afterwards was taken over by the Foreign Minister destined to be Prime Minister—and had another one "polished" in London, who is now employed in a fashionable club and still clings, as his best assets, to some of the dishes for which he has received a "polish", such as "No. 8" and "Most Precious Rice".

CHAPTER THREE

What is a Good Cook?

A GOOD cook, according to my idea, is one who is able to product at short notice an appetizing dish or meal with common materials at a minimum cost within a comparative short time:

1. At short notice. This implies that he is always fully prepared, knowing the subject from top to bottom and what to get as well as what can be got at a given season. He is also most likely a person of good temper, which is essential to good cooking, and one who has a good sense of management by having common materials always in stock to meet emergencies.

2. Appetizing dish or meal. This is of course a *sine qua non*: for unless he can do that he can have no claim to be a good cook.

3. Common materials. The mark of a good cook is that he is able to do what others cannot, like a Macaulay with his pen or a Rembrandt with his brush. To boil a cabbage or cauliflower and dish it after throwing the water away is not cooking. This is merely having the thing cooked and no more. But a good cook can turn even the commonest thing into a dish fit for a prince. There is a story that Emperor Chien Lung in his gay days of adventure *incognito* went into a wayside inn

one evening and asked for food. It happened that everything had been sold out or consumed, so that there was nothing left, except a sheet of rice that stuck to the bottom of the saucepan and was wholly browned like toast. The innkeeper at first did not know what to do but, being a good cook and suddenly remembering this remnant of rice in the saucepan, officered to make a nice dish out of this for the unexpected client. He turned it into a sort of rice broth with "crispy rice biscuits" made out of the "toasted" rice that remained in the saucepan and, with various seasonings, made it a very appetizing meal. The royal visitor was so delighted with it that, when he returned to the palace, he described the dish to his cook and ordered him to reproduce it. In time and through experiment the dish called "*Gaw Bar*", well liked by Westerners in China, was thus invented. It consists of highly flavoured soup served in a metal utensil over a small stand, inside which is a metal cup containing spirit. When everything is ready, the spirit is lit and when the soup begins to bubble, hot toasted rice, made in the form of biscuits, with the necessary seasonings, is poured into it like cornflakes. Thereupon a cheeping noise like the singing of a bird, causal by the absorption of the soup by the hot, toasted rice, comes from the utensil. This, together with the flame from the spirit burning underneath, presents a lively phenomenon, at once pleasing to the car and the eye and whetting one's appetite. Without further ado the soup with the toasted rice "biscuits" should be dished into each one's own bowl or soup plate. Delay would cause them to lose their crispness, which is one of the beauties of the dish. Compared with this, the practice of throwing bits of toast into the soup, as in the West, seems rather crude.

4. At a minimum cost. This is correlated with the last condition. A cook who always needs expensive materials or wastes a lot

can hardly be called a good cook, though he may do good cooking; for good cooking itself depends on how the cooking is done and not on the rarity, and therefore expensive nature, of the materials used. A good cook should be able to make even the commonest food tasty and appetizing. He would know how to make good use of materials and never wastes anything. Indeed he saves materials and expense. That is why good cooking, or the knowledge of it, is so important not only to the individual but also to the nation; because it contributes to national economy and national health. There used to be a saying, "What the English waste is enough to feed the Scotch people." What is wasted in America may be enough to help to feed half the world.

The truth that a person who can cook well is not necessarily a good cook may well be illustrated by a story that has the charm of being authentic. The father of a friend of mine, a gourmet, once borrowed the cook of a prominent and well-known man in Canton to prepare a dinner for entertaining some distinguished guests. The dinner was excellent, but the bill presented by the cook was about ten times the price one would have to pay at a restaurant for a similar meal. In view of the unusually large amount charged the cook was asked to render a detailed account of the materials used and the cost of each item. He did so the next day and the long account submit-

ted showed something like 20 chickens, 15 pigeons, 5 ducks, 2 hams, and half a pig! This recalls the story of the Prince de Soubise, whom his cook charged with fifty hams for a feast entertaining, perhaps, only a dozen guests. When the Prince saw the bill, he asked his cook whether he was out of his senses, saying: "Fifty hams? Do you want to feed all my regiment?"

"No, Your Highness," replied the cook, "there will only appear one on the table; but the others are not the less necessary for my concentrated gravy, my blonds, my trimmings, my . . ."[1]

What did my friend's father do? He paid; but in paying, I was told, he murmured, "We had a very good dinner no doubt, but we must have committed an unpardonable sin by sacrificing the lives of so many animals in order to gratify our appetite!"

The same cook accompanied his master to Malaya, where the latter was guest at the house of a man who had risen to be wealthy from a very humble station and together with his wife had seen hard times. One day the cook ordered fifty cabbages to be sent in. When they arrived, he just tore the heart out of each of them and threw the rest away. When the mistress of the house one morning caught sight of this huge heap of discarded cabbages, she asked what had happened to them. When told that the "famous" cook had required all these just to make one dish for his master, being a pious woman she was so horrified that she knelt down and prayed, "Almighty God, pardon me for this vicarious sin of waste!" "Vicarious", because by having such a guest with such a cook in her house she felt she bore some measure of indirect responsibility.

---

1. See *Physiology of Taste,* by J. A. Brillat-Savarin, p. 29.

5. Within a comparatively short time. This implies that the cook knows his job and knows it well. He knows exactly what to use and how it should be used and wastes no time. If you watch a Chinese cook cutting up meat or vegetables into fine bits, you cannot help marvelling at his skill and murmuring to yourself, "This is really a fine art!" Sometimes, you may also worry about his fingers, fearing that a slip of the sharp chopping-knife he is using may at any moment take off the tips of his fingers. A soprano insures her voice, and a professional dancer insures her feet, often for a very large sum. If the Chinese cook insures his fingers, the insurance company, should its representative see the insured's performance, would probably increase the premium, because the risk involved seems so great. But the Chinese cook thinks differently, because he knows his art. To watch him mincing meat on the chopping-board is to witness the performance of a knife-dance accompanied with music. You will see a pair of shining chopping-knives moving up and down swiftly and gracefully making continuous a noise that in tone is quite musical, e.g. "*Dig Dog, Dig Dog; Dig Dig, Dog Dog, Drig Drog, Drig Drog*", occasionally varied by a "*Ding Ding*" brought about by knocking one knife against the other. One may wonder why he does that. The answer is, he enjoys his job. His philosophy is simple: since he has to do his job he may just as well do it finely and, in order to do it finely, he makes it enjoyable too.

Indeed, this philosophy is the essence of good cooking itself. Since one must eat, one may just as well try to make eating an enjoyment. Thus, thanks to the genius of man, or rather of some men, good cooking had its origin. The poet with his pen, the artist with his brush, the cook with his chopping-knife — they all are alike in having one aim: to do a fine job.

A cook deserving to be called "good" must be able to prepare not only banquets but also what is generally known as "home cooking". In fact, the latter is more important than the former to the average home. One does not give banquets every day, but one must eat and eat daily and, in one's daily meal, it is the "home cooking" that is good for one's liver and health. Can there be such a person as a "Supercook"? Yes, such a cook is one who, apart from possessing all the qualifications of a good cook, is able to invent dishes and "cure" them when they have gone wrong; that is, improving their taste after they have been badly prepared. I have seen this done. For instance, when a dish already cooked is found to have a queer taste, the sauce is removed and a new one put in or other accessories are added, with the result that the undesirable taste is neutralized. If one can do that, he is a "Supercook".

It has been observed by a philosopher that "a people can have only the government it deserves"; so may it be said that a man can have only the cook he deserves. If he is indifferent to what he eats, his cook will in time also be indifferent to what he cooks, though he may be a good cook at the outset. To ensure that the cook will not deviate from his usual standard, one must show one's appreciation whenever it is due. Cooks, like any other men, are after all human. They can be encouraged, and will exert themselves without feeling the strains of the efforts made, when they see merits recognized and excellence appreciated. It is a saying of the West, "to cast pearls before swine"; in the East one says, "to play music to the cow". The idea of both is the same. However much one might offer to pay, no musician of repute would be willing to play a symphony to your pet cow, though out of curiosity he may do it just once in order to find out whether the animal, alleged to be music-loving, has more sense than its master!

CHAPTER FOUR

What is Good Cooking?

ONE is tempted to answer this question by saying "good cooking is what is produced by a good cook". This may seem to be
evading the question and be no definition at all. But when one
ponders over it one will find that it is not devoid of good sense;
for only a good cook can do good cooking. Many people who
ask this question often have in their minds what is good food.
This is quite a different matter and to give a comprehensive
answer would require volumes. With this observation good
cooking may be defined as "the employment of the process
of culinary art in producing what is appetizing to the eye, the
nose, and the palate, and agreeable to the stomach". That is,
when you see it, you like to smell it; when you smell it, you
like to taste it; when you taste it, you like to swallow it; and,
when you have swallowed it, you feel satisfied and gratified.
In particular, the food concerned is cooked to the right point
(as a rule neither underdone nor overdone); though rich, as
the case may be, but not too rich and never greasy; tender,
when it should be tender; crisp, when it should be crisp; and
unpredominated by the taste of anything added to or cooked
with it (such as sauce or accessories of any kind), unless this is
purposely intended (such as in making curry and the like), but
preserving in full, or to the largest extent possible, its original
flavour, whether it is meat, sea food, or vegetable. If by "good
cooking" is meant the food itself, as is often the case when
one says "this is good cooking" after having tasted the food,

the words "the employment of the process of the culinary art in producing" in the suggested definition should, of course, be omitted.

The conditions thus enumerated, I venture to think, apply equally to Chinese as well as non-Chinese food. At least this is the criterion by which I have judged Western food during my happy sojourn of more than a quarter of a century in the West. However, these few conditions, though they may seem commonplace to some, are quite exacting. Their fulfilment requires the active employment of the five senses, apart from skill, experience, and good judgment.

In Chinese food, in particular, there are certain specific terms describing that certain kinds of dishes, to be considered properly done, must fulfil certain conditions, e.g.:

1. *Huoo How* or, in Cantonese, *Faw How* (i.e. fire and time). It means that the proper degree of heat and the proper length of time should be used and applies specially to that class of dishes called *Duonn* or, in Cantonese, *Dun*, which is cooking by a double saucepan or by an earthenware utensil of a large size, containing a large quantity of materials, meat or poultry, with accessory ingredients. The cardinal idea is that the thing cooked should be tender without losing its original flavour. Therefore no large amount of water should be used, oth-

erwise you would be making soup out of the thing cooked; but a little of it should, if necessary, be added from time to time so as to prevent the thing cooked from getting dry or even burnt. This does not, of course, apply to cooking by a double saucepan, in which case you put enough water from the outset into the inner saucepan, because this will remain the same to the end; it is only necessary to add water to the outer saucepan from time to time when the water gets low. The next thing should be attended to in this form of cooking is the fire, which, after the initial stage, should continue to be low or just up to the simmering point; for hard boiling would destroy the intrinsic, delicate flavour of the thing cooked and cause its essence to become largely part of the juice or, in the case of cooking by a double saucepan, part of the soup, and, what's worse, to evaporate into the air.

The last point deserves notice in all forms of cooking. One, by experience, must have sometimes smelt an appetizing odour emitting from the kitchen. This agreeable smell will gradually diminish and ultimately disappear, particularly in cooking things like curry, unless care is taken to prevent it from escaping. The reason is simple. Taste in a given quantity of food has its maximum. If part of it is allowed to escape continually through evaporation, there will be a time when none will remain. To prevent this, hard boiling should be avoided after the initial stage, though in the case of cooking by a double saucepan the harm that may be done through hard boiling is not so great. Cooking in the way here suggested naturally takes longer time and requires more patience. But time and patience are essential to any achievement, no less in good cooking, which means so much to the pleasures of life and health.

2. *Walk He*. This is a Cantonese expression, meaning, literally, "the heat of the frying pan". It applies especially to that form of cooking called *Chow*, which is low-oil-quick-stir-frying, like cooking scrambled eggs but with more oil or fat, and above all, with rapid and successive movements of the hand in stirring the ingredients in the pan in the process of cooking. This form of cooking may be said to be unique in Chinese culinary art; because, as far as I know, no other nation, including the French, has any form of cooking equivalent to it. This is certainly a surprise, because it is a most delicate way of cooking all kinds of meat (cut in thin slices), vegetables (cut up, of course), and sea food susceptible of being cut into slices. No wonder the Chinese claim that they have the most advanced way of cooking as well as the best cuisine in the world; because, apart from being able to show a much greater variety of delicacies than any other nation, their means or forms of cooking are also more comprehensive, inasmuch as they have the equivalents of all forms of cooking employed by others and, in addition, some forms, like *Chow*, that are unknown to them.

Chow is a form of cooking very popular among the Chinese, especially the Cantonese. It does not require much time in actual cooking, but is a great test of skill in choosing, for instance, the right part of the meat (in the case of meat, one can use only the fillet or other tender parts;

[27]

in the case of poultry, one can use only the breast); in cutting it in the right way (i.e. it must be cut in cross vein); in using the right ingredients as accessories, which should be cut in more or less the same size as the principal, so that they will mix well, and should not exceed it in proportion, otherwise the taste of the accessories will be dominant; and, above all, in cooking the whole thing in the right way, having regard to the time, the fire, the seasoning, and other respects involved in the process. This may seem rather complicated but can in fact be easily learned except the part concerning actual cooking, which demands skill, so much so that when a new cook is employed on trial, he is chiefly judged, at least according to Cantonese custom, on the *Chow* dishes prepared by him. These "testing dishes", generally four of different kinds, are called by the Cantonese "Knocking-the-Door Bricks", meaning, metaphorically, the bricks used in primitive time by one, presumably having no right to enter the house, to knock down its door to effect an entry. If he succeeded, his object was attained. Similarly, if a cook on trial gets his four *Chow* dishes approved, he gets his employment.

It may be observed that cooking, however perfect, is good only to those who can appreciate what is good. To offer it to one who has an indifferent palate, having no idea of the time spent and the trouble involved in preparing it, is like offering an excellent cigar to one who smokes only cigarettes or delicious wine to one who drinks only beer. Once upon a time there was a well-known man in Peking who had a very good cook, particularly celebrated for cooking pig's tripe, called "*Chow Tsu Tu*", which is a Chinese delicacy and really delicious if well prepared. Whenever he gave a dinner one may be sure that this celebrated dish would figure in the menu. And when it was served, the cook would invariably secretly stand outside the dining-room listening to see whether any comment was made by the guests on his proud work of art. If no good comment was made by anyone, he would be so indignant that he would forthwith return to the kitchen, saying to his assistant something like this: "These people know nothing about good food. I am not going to waste my time. You cook the rest of the dinner." There and then went down his tool! As this "unofficial strike" must have happened more than once and became well known to the friends of his master, any of them happening to be among the guests, when that famous dish appeared on the table, would lavish on its exquisiteness favourable comments audible enough to be overheard by the cook sure to be standing outside listening. Out of appreciation or politeness such comments would certainly be echoed by the rest of the company. Thus the cook would be happy, the risk of a "strike" averted, and the excellence of the dishes that followed assured. If it happened that all the guests were strangers, the host himself would, on the appearance of the dish, tactfully draw their attention by prefacing it with words to this effect: "Now, let all of us have a drink and let me introduce to you a dish which has won the approval of all those who have honoured my table; I hope it will also win yours." Thereupon, a chorus of expressions of appreciation would break out and everybody would be happy, including the secret listener.

This incidentally shows that it is quite in order, nay, good manners, for the guests to praise at the table the food of the host, if he is a Chinese, and even talk about food in general as a topic of dinner conversation. There are also good reasons for such a convention; for, after all, food is at the time a subject of interest to all and it would be sheer hypocrisy to ignore it as if it were of no consequence. Moreover, certain dishes may require much time and skill to prepare. When they are perfectly done they are works of art. It would also be grossly unfair to the "artist" responsible and the host, merely to wash them down the throat one by one without a word of appreciation, like eating hurriedly something from a Snack Bar.

CHAPTER FIVE
Importance of Good Cooking

THE importance of good cooking can hardly be exaggerated. Apart from the pleasures it imparts to life, it can also promote friendship, smooth discussion or negotiation, and enhance domestic happiness. Dr. Johnson often took pride in saying that he could always smell a good dinner. If he could smell it, he would certainly enjoy it. When Boswell said to him that, if he were asked on the same day to dine with the first Duke in England and with the first man in Britain for genius, he should hesitate which to prefer, Johnson answered, "To be sure, sir, if you were to dine only once, and it were never to be known where you dined, you would choose rather to dine with the first man for genius."[1] By "genius" he must have included the man who is a genius in cooking. Thus one can see that, other things being equal, good cooking can help one to enlarge one's circle of friends and, through frequent association, thus rendered possible, to deepen one's friendship. In short, it plays a great part in social life. In the good old days of Peking that I knew, it was often through good cooking that one made friends. There were various "Dining groups" or "Wine groups", formed by people of different walks of life but of more or less equal standing, having, as their common object, good living and the promotion of friendship. They met weekly or fortnightly or on the occasion of the birthday of one of the members, who played host in turn. As a rule the din-

---

1. *Life of Dr. Johnson*, Vol. I, p. 274. Everyman Library ed.

ner was held in one's own home, unless for some reasons this was impracticable, in which case it could be held in a choice restaurant or, as was more often the case, in the house of a fellow-member, particularly if the latter had a good cook. On each occasion the host might include a couple of friends unknown to the others. Thus one made friends and was able also to keep friendship "in constant repair". Sometimes these gastronomic meetings were held for the promotion of art and literature. For instance, each member had to bring a picture or poem of his latest creation and submit it to the others for criticism. Though the primary object of these meetings was different, it was nevertheless good cooking that helped to maintain the continuity of interest and attendance. Above all, good fellowship and good understanding were fostered or enhanced.

As to the part that cooking can play in smoothing discussion or negotiation, this must be a common or common-place experience of every man of affairs. Millions change hands in commercial transactions yearly as a sequel to a good lunch or a good dinner, and "Will you lunch with me at − −?"[1] is a familiar phrase in the business world either in prefacing a successful transaction or in celebrating one. Without good cooking it is certain that Boswell would not have succeeded in "enticing" Dr. Johnson to meet Jack Wilkes — a triumph commended by Edmunds Burke as "Nothing equal to it in the whole history of the *Corps Diplomatique*". As has been remarked in the Preface, no great event in history ever happened without its being previously planned or determined at a feast. Be sure that, in order that the feast should be successful, the cook must have been warned that special care should be taken to make it a good meal. Men, after all, are human, whether they are princes or peasants, poets or politicians, phi-

---

1. A restaurant known for good food, of course.

losophers or physicians. They must eat, and good cooking, agreeable both to the palate and the stomach, will put them in good humour and in a more reasonable frame of mind, thus opening the way to a fruitful discussion. Indeed, bad cooking has helped to change the course of history. Napoleon felt so bad after eating badly cooked lamb that he made tactical errors which lost him the decisive battle of Leipzig.

It is well known that the office of the Lord Mayor of London entails a great deal of entertainment, so much so that hospitality at the Guildhall with its traditional turtle soup is proverbial, and that no person, though qualified, can "afford" to accept the honour of that office unless he is wealthy. One may wonder why he has to do all this and do it so elaborately. Some may say that it is to keep up a tradition. Such an explanation would be telling only half the tale; for no tradition would be kept up for so long at so great an expense, unless it has a practical value which is as good today as it was yesterday. The true answer is that, being a successful business man, as all Lord Mayors are, he knows the value of a good dinner, particularly in the promotion of good will and of all that follows. One Lord Mayor, who lived at the time when England was threatened with a grave constitutional crisis over the power of the House of Lords concerning Money Bills, even thought that the advantage of a dinner, provided, I sup-

pose, the cooking was good, might have averted the crisis. Let his words be quoted:

"My few observations on the value of dining really arose out of some remarks that were made by the gentleman who proposed the toast of the Corporation and my health. He seemed rather to infer that one of the principal functions of the Corporation was that of dining. In reply I was unable to accept all that suggestion implied, yet ventured to submit that the art of dining was, after all, within proper limits, a very valuable agency for obtaining, under genial conditions, agreements and settlements not so easily or effectively obtained under more austere circumstances. After all, the question of dining is human, and if we are to achieve results, however laudable, by human agency, surely we are justified in adopting methods which are common to all, and which, speaking generally, appeal to the whole of the people."[1]

This is only good sense and demonstrates a homely truth that must have been daily experienced in various degrees by men of affairs. I actually know a person in London who gives a series of dinners every year at a well-known hotel with the best of food to representatives of different nations, with no other object, as I was told, than the promotion of international peace, believing that, by bringing them together in genial surroundings and thus setting them the example of goodwill, goodwill will be fostered, leading to the fulfilment of his pious wish. He may not have succeeded yet, but he certainly deserves success. The cynic may say that this is putting an excessive value on dining. But no less an institution than the "World Court" at the Hague, of which I had the honour of being a member before and during the Second World War,

---

1. Reported in the London *Evening News*.

would, before the commencement of the proceedings of a case and in the name of its President, give, in honour of the representatives of the parties, an elaborate banquet to which all the judges, including senior members of the Registry and the counsel of both parties, were invited. This is no mere courtesy and can only mean that it is thought that this is a civilized way of introducing a judicial combat compatible with the dignity of a World Tribunal, with the hope that the good feelings thus engendered will enhance, in the minds of the parties in dispute, the realization that, though they are at the moment in litigation, they are in fact co-operating in the common task of promoting international peace, inasmuch as the very submission of their disputes to the Court for decision is *ipso facto* a friendly gesture and a testimony of their will to settle disputes by pacific means instead of going to war, as they might in the old days.

This custom of the "World Court" recalls a usage in vogue in *traditional China* since time immemorial, but more profound in purpose. It actually settles the dispute over steaming-hot dishes or appetizing dainty refreshments and hot tea, at the expense not of a law court but of a Chamber of Commerce, a guild, or a third party, as the case may be. Most disputes are settled in this way. Thus, instead of going to litigation, which, according to a well-known Queen's Counsel of the English Bar after "forty years' experience", is nothing but vanity, people seek a decision truly "by their peers". Such a procedure or means of achieving a settlement minimizes bitterness, if any, of an adverse decision. It saves time and expense in costs and in lawyer's fees, which in modern litigations is often so enormous as to make justice almost prohibitive.

My readers may say, "I can quite understand the value of 'steaming-hot dishes', but why refreshments and hot tea?" All China tea, with its hundreds of varieties, is a delightful beverage. It not only quenches thirst, including thirst for quarrels, but also cools temper, though it is drunk hot; while Chinese refreshments, made of flour or rice powder in scores of forms with minced meat and various other ingredients, such as bamboo shoot, mushroom, shrimp, Chinese cabbage of different types, water chestnut, etc., are so dainty and delicious that no normal being while eating such food would be inclined to be quarrelsome. They form part of the Chinese cuisine and their making is an art. Try some in a Chinese restaurant and you will understand better what I mean.

What has good cooking to do with domestic happiness? It has a lot. As pointed out by a poet and quoted in the Preface, "*We may live without books, but a civilized man cannot live without cooks.*" In the average home under modern conditions, the cook is probably the wife. Imagine a young man and a young woman falling in love, and then sealing their romance by getting married. This opens a new chapter of life, the formation of a home, giving rise to duties, of which none is more important than cooking, because it is a daily affair. In China this duty is performed by the bride three days after the wedding, as instanced by the following classical poem:

"She tours the kitchen three days after wedding,
And cleans her hands to do the homely cooking.
For knowing not the taste of husband's mother,
She gives a bit first to his little sister."

The last two lines show devotion, tact, and intelligence, necessitated by the fact that, at least in the old days, people, though married, lived with their parents. But let us suppose that the couple have a home of their own, as is generally the case today. The husband, a decent fellow, goes to work early in the morning and comes home late in the evening after a day's toil. Hungry, tired, and perhaps half frozen on a wintry night, he looks forward, as it is also fair, to a good meal. And suppose he finds on the table, though nicely set, only slices of cold meat or something partly burnt on a cold plate. What a disappointment! Being hungry, he has to swallow what he can find. But, probably, after a few mouthfuls he lays down his knife and fork. The wife, perhaps, still feeling the pain of a wounded finger due to a slip of the carving-knife, or because she pulled hurriedly the burning meat out of the oven, may glance at him and say anxiously, "Dear, have you no appetite?" Embarrassed and confused, but tender to his bride, he may just answer, "Darling, I am not very hungry." Yet he knows he is not telling the truth and, being a good Christian, feels at once a prick in his conscience. But such a state of things cannot go on for ever. It will, in time, lead to indigestion, ill health, and nervous breakdown, giving rise to bad temper and, perhaps, ending in a complaint of incompatibility of temperament.

Let us change the picture. Suppose, instead of something icy cold or hall-burnt, he finds something steaming-hot and appetizing to the eye, the nose, and the palate. How delightful! What would he say? Imagine the following dialogue:

"My pearl," says the husband, "I knew everything you touched would turn into gold, but I never thought you were such a good cook. This is better than anything I have ever tasted!"

"Really!" replies the wife. "I am so pleased! In fact I did this only the first time."

"Wonderful!" says the husband. "You remember, dearie, the dinner we had together at the Waldorf (or the Ritz as the case may be) on the occasion of your last anniversary. It was very good, as you said at the time and often afterwards; but it cannot be compared with this by a long way!"

Being human, the wife cannot help feeling the compliment, but modesty, inherent in a woman, obliges her to say: "This is impossible. I have, in fact, never learned any cooking."

"Sweet," replies the husband, "this is so much the more to your credit; you are a genius; you are a born cook; your talents are natural gifts which cannot be acquired or equalled!"

"What an eloquence you have, dear, tonight!" interjected the wife. And not knowing what else to say, she changes the subject. "Let me give you a little of the brown . . . a little of the stuffing . . . some gravy . . . a squeeze of this orange; . . . or the lemon, perhaps, may have more zest." (Here the language is borrowed from Boswell in describing how Jack Wilkes tried to please Dr. Johnson when they dined together the first time.)

"Be careful, honey," says the husband, "don't let the gravy get on to your pretty dress. Allow me to do it."
"No, dear," answers the wife, "you have had your day's toil; you have done your part. This is now my turn!"

"My dearest," utters the husband, "you are a perfect wife. When we have a couple of children, you will be a perfect mother and we shall have a perfect home!"

The young wife may blush at this remark, but the colours thus brought to her cheeks can only make her look more lovely, and it is more than likely that they will have twins at the first instance! Isn't this domestic happiness? And isn't it important to know good cooking?

CHAPTER SIX

Schools of Cooking in China

AS CHINA is like a continent, at least larger than Europe, it is only to be expected that her food cannot be quite the same throughout the country, just as in Paris one can dine Alsatian, Bearnaise, Provençal, Savoyarde, etc. In China there must be hundreds, if not thousands, of ways of preparing food. Every district, not to say province, has some special dishes of its own. Yet, when one comes to classification, all the forms and styles of cooking, in the proper sense of the term, can be grouped under five Schools, namely Canton, Fukien, Honan, Shantung, and Szechuen. Perhaps Yang Chow and Kiangsu may be added, though the former is more renowned for its refreshments than for its dishes, except a few, of which "Lion's Head"—a form of meat ball—is best known and most delicious. Other provinces may have their own ways of cooking, of which some can be good, but which can hardly claim to form a distinct School; for they are in nature not very different from those of one or another of the "Big Five". By "ways of cooking" are not meant particular dishes, which every province, nay, every district, may have, and of which some are very tasty; but they are too isolated to be dignified with the word "School", and in fact they are generally a form of home cooking, never to appear in what may be called a banquet. It is, however, proverbial that one man's food is another man's poison, so it is possible that a person accustomed to the food of one School may prefer it to that

of another School. I feel it, therefore, "diplomatic" in listing the five Schools to put them
in alphabetical order. Nevertheless, there is a
saying in China, "To be born in Soo Chow, to
eat in Kwang Chow (i.e. Canton), to dress in
Hang Chow, and to die in Leou Chow." For
Soo Chow is known for beauty, Canton for
food, Hang Chow for silk, and Leou Chow for
wood for making coffins. Besides, by far the
majority of the Chinese restaurants abroad
are Cantonese. Though this may be due to the
fact that most of the Chinese abroad are Cantonese, I think it is also due to the fact that
Cantonese cooking is broader in basis and can
be "international" in taste. Canton has also,
at its disposal, a greater variety of sea food,
fresh or preserved (i.e. dried in the sun), than
any other province, and so has the advantage of creating more dishes than any of the
other Schools. Therefore it is only fair to put
the Canton School at the top. Of course, every
School has its specialities which other Schools
cannot equal, and, however excellent a School
may be, it has its excessives or defects. Having tasted the cooking of all these Schools for
an almost even period of time for each, and
so being in a position to say that my taste is
"cosmopolitan", I venture to express the opinion that the Canton School, though it may err,
errs rather on the right side either by making
some dishes a little too rich or by crowding
too many good things into one feast.

Though there are different Schools, whose methods of preparation and tastes are distinct, they are common in using more or less the same accessory ingredients, such as bamboo shoot, mushroom, and other vegetables; the same principles, such as *Chow*, grill, fry, stew, etc.; the same fat, such as peanut oil and sometimes pork fat or chicken fat, but never butter or other animal fat; and the same sauce, the soya, but never tomato and the like. Therefore it is only to a Chinese there can appear any difference in the cooking; to a foreigner, unless he has long been in China and has often tasted the cooking of different Schools, all would appear the same — Chinese food and Chinese cooking.

Why is the best cooking confined only to five or six provinces? Canton owes it largely to the existence of a leisure class, descendants of people who became rich after the port was thrown open to foreign trade, to the fact that it is blessed with a great variety of sea food of the first quality, and to the discovery of the ingenious method of preserving sea food by having it salted and then dried in the sun. People of the leisure class used to rival with one another in taking pride in possessing the best cook or in inventing new dishes. Even now in Hong Kong almost every distinguished club claims that its own cook can prepare certain dishes which no restaurant or other clubs can produce to the same excellence. This is somewhat a relic of the leisure life that once prevailed in Canton in the good old days. Fukien probably owes it to the fact that it produces the best soya sauce and, certainly, to the fact that it possesses a long sea coast, which supplies it with an abundance of sea food. A people who know how to make good sauce is bound to understand good living; for sauce is, after all, made only to make food tasty. If a people is particular even about the accessory, it is only logical that it will be more so about the principal—the food itself. As regards soya sauce, what is made by the Cantonese is also very good but not so rich as that made in Fukien.

Honan owes it to the fact that it was once the capital, which being the seat of the Court was alone enough to create the urge for good cooking. Szechuen, though it has never been the capital of the whole country, has more than once been the seat of an independent government, and what applies to Honan must be applicable to Szechuen likewise. Besides, it has the richest soil with variable climates for the production of a great variety of natural products, including numerous kinds of fungus, some of which, like truffles, are delicacies.

Shantung, apart from having been capital of different States in the pre-Christian era, owes it to the fact that it is the native land of the ancient sages, notably Confucius and Mencius, whose cultural influence must have had an effect on its food, if food has anything to do with culture, as has been discussed in the Introduction. Though Peking has been the capital for several centuries, the province of which it forms part produces no cooking of its own. It adopts the Shantung School, probably because most of the people engaged in the more important forms of trade in that province come from Shantung. This also speaks for the fact that the Shantung School has had great opportunity of improving, if not perfecting, its art of cooking.

Yang Chow owes it to the discovery of salt mines which brought great wealth to a large number of persons, then known as "salt merchants", who, having the means to indulge themselves in good living, created the demand for good food and good cooking, so much so that Canton, though it can claim now to have the best cuisine, owes at least one dish, called "*Chow Fan*" (fried rice), well loved by Westerners, and most of the delicious refreshments, notably the egg noodles, to Yang Chow. Until the beginning of the Republic Cantonese restaurants still labelled their noodles and fried rice as "Yang Chow Noodles" and "Yang Chow *Chow Fan*". But the Cantonese, being themselves clever in the culinary art, soon improved what they had copied from others and have since created a number of refreshments unequalled even by the Yang Chow School, except, I think, what are called "*Shau May*" (a form of meat packet), "*Guann Tang Bow*" (a form of meat bun with soup inside), and "*Tang Yuen*" (a form of flour ball with sweet inside), in which the Yang Chow School excels.

THE CANTON SCHOOL

This School has a greater variety of dishes than any other School for reasons already given, and because the Cantonese are keen in creating new dishes and eat a number of delicacies which people of other provinces do not know or may not eat at all, such as frog legs, turtles of different categories, certain kinds of games, etc. For instance, Northern people as a rule would not eat turtles, and even pigeons, which they call "holy birds". An old friend of mine, who has been Ambassador to the United States and the United Kingdom and is now living in retirement, told me this story. When he was Commissioner in Harbin in pre-Republican days, he had a cook who was very fond of gambling. Whenever he had pigeons for his meal he knew that the cook had lost money. Why? Because few people there, at least in those days, would eat pigeons, which were therefore very cheap! Another story is about frog legs. Farmers in Fukien used to engage much in litigation against one another for throwing over others' fields frogs found in their own, apparently without realizing that these animals are very helpful in destroying insects for the benefit of the crop. One day the Viceroy of the province, who happened to be a Cantonese, heard of this and ordered the frogs to be brought to him. As soon as people learned that His Excellency made a good feast of these once troublesome creatures, all litigations of this nature ceased and frogs gained their "passports" to the domain of delicacies.

Food of the Canton School as a rule costs more, partly because it always uses highly concentrated chicken bouillon as the basis of soup and cooking in general, and partly because it is apt to use expensive materials, considered or reputed to have special properties of nutrition. In making soups, such as chicken broth and, particularly, turtle soup, it often uses certain herbs possessing some medical value, considered to be specially good for one's health. In consequence people sometimes would say that the Cantonese are fond of using medicines in their cooking. The fact is, these herbs enhance the taste of the soup and are used instead of sugar to add sweetness to it. That those, or some of them, are also used as medicine is, in most cases, a coincidence. It excels, for instance, in *Chow*, (low-oil-quick-stir-frying) dishes, in soup, especially turtle soup, in roasting or grilling pork or poultry, in steamed dishes, in *Duonn* (cooked in a double saucepan or large earthenware) dishes, in making "plain-cooked" chicken, and, particularly, in preparing shark's fin — an art no other School can equal — as well as in most forms of dainty refreshments.

THE FUKIEN SCHOOL

It is good fairly all round and its food is noted for its lightness and taste. Its soup, in particular, is tasty and clear, so clear that, in the process of making it so, some essence may sometimes have unconsciously been taken away. It is also fond, or rather a little too fond, of making soupy dishes, so that in a feast of twelve dishes a quarter of these may belong to that category. For a banquet it cannot be compared with the Canton School in variety, richness, or grandeur.

THE HONAN SCHOOL

Its food in general is richer than that of the Fukien School. It specializes rather than generalizes and so its dishes, though limited, generally maintain a high and uniform standard. It is specially noted for "Sweet and Sour Sauce" dishes and for cooking "Yellow River carps", "One Fish in Four Forms", "Walnut Kidney", Custard in the form of "Norwegian Omelette", "Monkey Head" mushrooms (which grow on trees exclusively in Honan and taste better even than truffles, so prized in French cuisine), and bear's paw, of which the preparation may puzzle the cooks of other Schools. In frying kidney, cut in the size of half a walnut, the Honan cook dips it in boiling oil and takes it out alternately. Thus it does not shrink much in the process of cooking and tastes tender and crisp at the same time.

The Shantung School

Like the Honan School it does not generalize and so maintains a uniform standard. Its known dishes in a restaurant do not exceed, perhaps, a score, and its food, as a whole, can be said to be light. It is noted for dishes prepared with "wine stock", for "soft-frying" dishes, for grilled duck—the famous "Peking duck"—and for swan's liver cooked in "wine stock", which tastes as delicious as *foie gras*. It is remarkable that it has hardly any *Chow* dishes.

The Szechuen School

This School has, perhaps, a greater variety of dishes than the last two Schools discussed. It is noted for hot-taste dishes which are very appetizing, for ham, probably because it is

near Yunnan which produces the best ham, for various dishes composed of fungus that grow in Szechuen, for certain vegetable dishes prepared with chicken fat, for the dish known as "Chicken Blood", and for frying chicken meat wrapped in paper. Its cooking is fairly representative but is inclined to be oily.

THE KIANGSU AND YANG CHOW SCHOOL

The noted dishes of this School are "*Chow* Shrimps", "Lion's Head" (a form of meat ball in the size of a tangerine), "*Chow* Eel" in thin slices, "*Guann Shi*" (i.e. bean curd cut in small slices and prepared with highly tasty broth together, sometimes, with small slices of mushroom and bamboo shoot), ham, crab, and "*Hung Shau*" fish (i.e. fish, after it has been fried a bit, cooked over a simmering fire with wine, soya sauce, and a touch of garlic, ginger, spring onion, and just enough water to make gravy, preferably added to the pan little by little until the fish is cooked).

There is, however, one School which is worthy of being mentioned — that is, the "Vegetarian School". In some temples one often finds some extremely tasty and cleverly done vegetarian dishes, made of "bean curd skin" (i.e. bean curd as thin as paper seasoned with soya sauce and dried) and made artistically in the forms of "ham", "duck", "chicken", or "fish". Vegetarian substitutes are found even for such delicacies as shark's fin and "bird's nest". Vegetarian soup can also be made to taste like chicken broth. It consists of soup made from sprouts of the soya beans. This form of cooking is a distinct art, which often draws admiration from foreigners. In Shanghai there are several vegetarian restaurants and a vegetarian feast at some of them can be as expensive as a luxurious dinner at one of the non-vegetarian restaurants.

CHAPTER SEVEN

Classification of Dishes

DISHES, according to their nature, taste, or ways of cooking or preparation, may be classified into:

1. International and National.
2. National and Regional.
3. Formal or Banquet cooking and Informal or Home cooking.

By "International" is not meant here that the particular dish is actually common to more than one nation. It may be, for the time being, exclusive to only one nation. For cooking, though an art, is in some respects also a science, which is common to all: its temporary exclusiveness, though it earns a laurel for the nation creating it, does not make it "National", so long as it embodies no acquired taste, just as the fact that the Hydrogen bomb can now be manufactured only by the United States does not make the bomb "National". But in order to be classified as "International" the dish must fulfil two conditions:

1. The very thing used is generally what is consumed as food by people of different countries, such as egg, poultry, beef, mutton, pork, various kinds of known sea food or vegetables, and the like.

2. The way of cooking it is more or less common to other peo-

ples, such as baking, boiling, frying, grilling, roasting, steaming, stewing, and the like, and it is not so prepared as to carry a taste that is "acquired", or, though the way of cooking is peculiar to a particular people, its taste is more or less common to all people.

The realization of this is important especially in entertainment between people of the Occident and the Orient. For instance, if a Chinese entertains an American or an Englishman who has never tasted Chinese food before, and offers him what the Chinese people consider to be a national delicacy, the chance is that his guest may not relish it. In this the French are more enterprising. In the '30s a distinguished Frenchman representing the League of Nations visited me in Nanking and had lunch with me. He was given, *inter alia*, "Minced dried Oyster, *low-oil quick-stir-fried* with minced pork and water chestnut", a delicacy of the birth district of Dr. Sun Yat-Sen, Founder of the Chinese Republic, and therefore a "Regional" and not even a "National" dish of the Chinese. It must have been the first time that he had ever had such food, but he liked it so much that he said he had never tasted anything so delicious before. Another time, I entertained a Frenchman at the Hague with shark's fin. As he evidently enjoyed it, I said it was supposed to be good for children, because it contained a high percentage of calorie, protein, calcium, and phosphorus.[1] He replied, "It is very good for grownup people too!" This is rather typical of his race, but with others it may not be the same. Once a gentleman of a well-known London journal was offered, *inter alia*,

1. In 100 grammes, as scientifically analysed, it contains calorie 384; protein 89.4 gm.; fat 2 gm.; carbohydrate 1 gm.; calcium 111 mg.; phosphorus 141 mg. See *Composition of Foods Used in Far Eastern Countries*, by Woot-Tsuen Wu Leung, R. K. Pecot, and B. K. Watt. Agricultural Handbook No. 34. Bureau of Human Nutrition and Home Economics. U.S. Dept of Agriculture, 1952. Complete protein contains 24 amino Acids, of which 18, particularly rich in Lysine, are believed to be found in shark's fin.

this dish. He asked what it was. On receiving the answer that it was shark's fin, he murmured, "I wish I had not been told!" and, only after his editorial colleague, sitting next to him, had said it was very good, ate it with fortitude!

However, it is always advisable to offer to your foreign friends, if you are not sure of their taste, not your "national" delicacies but dishes of an "international" nature, as understood here. A Swiss, for instance, would not offer *fondus* to his foreign guests the first time he entertains them. In this respect the Chinese cuisine is much more fortunate than any other including even the French; because it has a much greater variety of things to offer in its many, many ways of cooking eggs, meat, poultry, game, ham, fish, noodles, rice, and vegetables. All these dishes, which run into hundreds in form, are "international" both in nature and in taste. For example, who would say that the famous "Peking duck" is not within this category? It is peculiar to the Chinese only in the sense that it is unrivalled in flavour and only the Chinese can produce it. Moreover, since the Chinese generally use in their cooking peanut oil, which is neutral in taste and therefore cannot offend the palates of people of any race or religion, Chinese food, except the special "national" delicacies, is, like Chinese philosophy, such as "Within the four seas all are brothers", essentially "international" and can appeal to all, though its way of preparation may be different. Western cuisines, however, are not in such a happy position, because they use butter, which, having a predominant taste of its own, is alien to the taste of practically all Eastern people and thus gives the food a "national" character *vis-à-vis* the latter, though, of course, "international" among Western nations.

By "National", as contrasted with "Regional", is here meant

not that the dish concerned is commonly or "nationally" eaten by a certain people, like roast beef to the English or the American, which is "national" in a different sense, but that it is common and peculiar to a particular nation, like shark's fin to the Chinese, *escargot* to the French, *fondus* to the Swiss, whale steak to the Norwegians, raw sea food to the Japanese, and the like. In short, it covers all the special delicacies of a particular cuisine. Roast beef, though a national food of the British or the Americans, is, in fact, "international" in character, as understood here; because it fulfils the two conditions above described. "Regional" dishes are those that are prepared in a way peculiar to the people of a particular district. Some of them may be "international" in nature and some of them may be excellent in taste, but they generally partake of a less urban character and so rarely find their way to the banquet table outside the district to which they belong. Such dishes in China must number by the hundreds, if not by the thousands; for the Chinese in general are so fond of good living, as already discussed, that every district is bound to be able to show some distinct dishes of its own. It is, therefore, worth while, even for a Chinese who loves good food, to try some of the known dishes of every district where he may happen to be.

The distinction between Formal or Banquet cooking and Informal or Home cooking must

exist somewhat in every country which has a known cuisine, and the finer the cuisine, perhaps, the greater the distinction. The former means those dishes, or kinds of dishes, which, generally speaking, one eats only at a feast and no one would like to eat every day, good though they are, or which are too complicated in preparation to be cooked in an ordinary home, or of which the preparation is such as is characteristic of food one finds at a restaurant. In all cases special emphasis is laid on form and presentation, and the food, as a rule, tends to be rich. The latter, however, is just the reverse. It is the daily food, though it varies. It is simple in form, though the preparation may require skill. It is never "mass production" but always specially prepared. It may have "less art" but certainly have "more substance". It may consist of materials so common that it can never climb to the banquet table, yet it is so appetizing and tasty that it would be missed if too long absent from the daily meal. China is rich in this kind of cooking. Even those provinces, whose food may not be of such a standard as to form a distinct School, and, particularly, Kiangsu, Chekiang, and Anhwei, have in various degrees certain good home cooking — a special art of the maid-cook, if not the housewife. In this Canton is, of course, on a higher scale, thanks to its great variety of sea food, fresh or dried (i.e. preserved), to the high quality of its poultry (of which some are fed with special food; in Hong Kong some are fed with milk), to its many kinds of vegetable, of which some are not found elsewhere, to its many ways of preparation, and to the fondness of its people for good cooking. To taste the food of a Cantonese family known for home cooking is quite a pleasant change from what one eats at a restaurant, however excellent the latter may be. Here again this is often the case of the triumph of the unprofessional female cook rather than the regular *chef*.

CHAPTER EIGHT

Instances of Special Chinese Delicacies and Their Preparation

CHINESE delicacies are so numerous that it is impossible to embody more than a fraction of them in a volume and still less in one chapter. Besides, this is not meant to be a cookery book or a book of recipes, which any professional book can more or less furnish, but one primarily intended to introduce to the Western world the Chinese cuisine and that aspect of Chinese culture with which it is associated, and, incidentally, to discuss some fundamental principles which underlie Chinese cooking and, *mutatis mutandis*, good cooking in general. Therefore just a few of those delicacies that are best known and peculiar to the Chinese are dealt with here.

It is no secret that people unfamiliar with the Chinese cuisine are apt to think that the Chinese people eat a lot of "odd" things, so much so that the word "chinoiserie" is applied to their food no less than to other things Chinese. But what one people thinks it odd to eat may well appear to another to be odd not to eat. For instance, Eastern people in general would think it odd that Western people should like high game, such as grouse or pheasant in its right state, or high cheese, such as stilton or gorgonzola at its best, and the latter would think it odd that the former should be shy about these, excellent as they are to those accustomed to Western delicacies. This, in principle, applies to every rare delicacy of one *cuisine vis-à-vis* another. Caviar of the Russians or Roumanians and *foie gras* of the French, so relished by the elect, would form no exception, if they had not been so well known in Western societies. Therefore, there is nothing very extraordinary in that the Chinese should like shark's fin, "Bird's Nest", and other "odd" things, which often only mean delicacies undiscovered. The shark, indeed, is a very ferocious animal, but its fin must be most harmless and the cleanest part of a fish. Well prepared, it is not only most delicious to the palate but also most wholesome to the system, because of the high percentage of calorie, protein, calcium, and phosphorus it contains, as already mentioned in the preceding chapter. It is the same with "Bird's Nest". The word "nest" is, perhaps, misleading. Some people may imagine that "Bird's Nest Soup" is soup made simply from a bird's nest pulled down from a tree grown, perhaps, in one's own garden, boiled in water with or without the bird or its young, and then served with pepper and salt! The Chinese, who have survived for thousands of years and have contributed so many fundamental discoveries and inventions to the world, should be credited with a better sense than that. The so-called "Bird's Nest" is no more and no less than predigested protein from some kind of sea weed gathered from the sea not by the ordinary swallows as commonly believed, but by a particular specie of petrel of the *Procellariidae* family, living not on land but along the cliffs of the Pacific islands and digested by the alkaline fluid of the mouths of these birds before using it for building their nests. As food it possesses a delicate flavour, which will be brought out by a tasty *bouillon*, and is specially rich in protein,[1] particularly good for those who suffer from ulcerated stomach, as evidenced by Dr. Cotui's recent discovery of the use of predigested protein for the treatment

---

1. 94.3 gm. in 100 grammes. See *Composition of Foods used in Far Eastern Countries, supra.*

of that ailment. After all, Chinese taste for rare delicacies is by no means isolated. It finds a counterpart in the menu of a no less known restaurant than the Sports Afield Club, New York City, such as:

Mexican Armadillo (for 4)	$100.00
Beaver & Beaver Tail	27.00
South American Boar	18.00
Caribou	75.00
Australian Kangaroo	50.00
Muskrat	62.00
Porcupine	55.00
Ostrich Eggs	35.00
Water Buffalo	13.00

Judged by the prices charged, these must be highly regarded as delicacies. With this observation, what are relished by the Chinese may now be discussed.

I. SHARK'S FIN.

It is produced in India, Korea, Japan, Mexico, Norway, Venezuela, and the Philippines. That produced by the last named country is the best, called "Manila Yellow", because of its colour, and the most expensive too; but it also contains more eatable portion, apart from being more tender and richer in taste. No doubt, wherever sharks are found, there is the fin; but if the people there do not know how to preserve or cure it by having it dried in the sun after they have caught the shark, they miss a valuable trade. Curiously enough, it has no taste when it is fresh. It becomes tasty only after it has been preserved or cured and afterwards restored to its original state.

Its preparation requires the following stages:

(It is presumed that the fin is raw and made for one conventional portion—that is, one dish, *inter alia*, for 10-12 persons. Use about 3 lb. such fin).

(*a*) Soak it in cold water for 3 days in order to get it softened. This is advisable, because it will enable the process employed in the (*b*) stage to get a better result. But if you are pressed for time, you may proceed to stage (*b*) from the very beginning.

(*b*) Simmer it for 4-5 hours or rather until its sandy skin comes off or becomes easily detachable and the decayed bone hidden in the meat at the top of the fin can also be easily removed. If not, simmer it a little longer. But do not boil it hard. At this stage the process is only to prepare it for cleaning. During this process a rather unpleasant odour is bound to emit from the water. This comes from the decayed meat and bone at the top of the fin and not from the fin itself, which is absolutely clean and odourless. Therefore the water should be changed every fifteen minutes during the first hour and every thirty minutes during the subsequent hours, in order to get rid of the unpleasant odour and to prevent the fin from being affected by it. During this process the fin will gradually reveal itself in transparent colour and curl from its original triangular shape into the form of a crescent. When it has been sufficiently simmered and is ready for cleaning, proceed to the next stage.

(c) Rub off any sandy skin that may remain, remove the bone, if any, and chip off any meat that is not absolutely white or firm. Any bone or any yellowish (i.e. decayed) meat, if left, would spoil the whole thing, because it has an unpleasant odour. The fin can be said to be clean and ready for cooking when it has absolutely no *decaying* smell. In the course of cleaning take care to keep the fin compact as much as possible and not to break it up; for the more compact the fin the better its presentation. In restaurants a dish of compact shark's fin, called *Bow Chyh*, costs at least three times more than one of loose shark's fin. For this reason the Cantonese cook uses a net made of bamboo to fasten the fin in the course of preparation at the (d) and (e) stages in order to keep the fin compact or in good shape—a device unknown to the cooks of other Schools.

But this device is not really ideal; for the bamboo net, however clean it may be, might, in the long process of cooking at the *(e)* stage, leave, at least psychologically, a trace (however infinitesimal it may be) of the taste of the bamboo. Anyhow, such a net might hinder the juices of the ingredients cooked with the fin from permeating the fin thoroughly. Therefore a net made of fine silver wire should be used.

However, only fin of a high quality can be kept compact at all, because it contains a high percentage of gelatine. Fin of a poor quality loosens itself after the *(b)* stage, for which reason this kind of fin is generally cooked, in a soupy form, with chicken or crab meat, as hereafter described.

(d) Assuming that the fin is now absolutely clean and ready for semi-final or final cooking, simmer it again for three-quarters of an hour with two slices of green ginger, a few pieces of spring onion (or one cut-up onion), and one glass of wine like sherry, changing the water twice. This is to get rid of the last trace of the "fishy" taste of the fin — not the unpleasant odour, which at this stage is assumed to be entirely absent. Note that the fin is still far from being in an eatable state.

(e) Now comes the final or rather semi-final stage. Put the fin in a *double saucepan* together with a quarter pound of ham and pork (both of which should be partly fat and partly lean) and the meat of one fresh chicken. Add a glass of wine like sherry and two cups of water. Then cook the whole thing over a medium fire for about three hours, or rather until the fin is quite tender. The latter condition is essential, otherwise the fin is not fit for eating yet. But it should not be overdone, otherwise the fin would partly melt into jelly, though it is better to err on the right side.

(f) Finally, assuming the fin is tender enough for eating, take it out carefully from the double saucepan without loosening any part of it, if possible (assuming it is compact), and put it into a pan without the juice or any of the ingredients used in the (e) stage. Pour over it the highly concentrated *bouillon*, already and separately prepared by having one whole cut-up fresh chicken and about three ounces of cut-up lean ham cooked *without water* in a *double saucepan*. (This *bouillon* is about two cupfuls, after the chicken and ham have been thus cooked for three hours over a medium fire, and is highly tasty, because it is really chicken and ham essence.) Then cook the whole thing again for ten minutes over a low fire, so that this new juice may penetrate into the fin. Add one teaspoonful of soya sauce. Taste the juice before adding any salt; for the ham may have made the fin and juice salty enough. It should then be served in a very hot dish without any delay. This final process should never take place until the guests are ready for the dish. Therefore, when the (e) stage is completed, the fin may be dished up and put away in a cool place for the final process to be applied when required.

It may be asked why the final process is needed, since, after the (e) stage, the fin is really in an eatable state and the juice must be very tasty too, thus saving also the expense of another chicken and an extra bit of ham. The answer is that the juice yielded in the (e) stage is a little "messy", being mixed with the jelly resulting from part of the fin melted, and not so sharp in taste as the fresh concentrated chicken and ham essence. Economy has no place in the realm of delicacies.

N.B. — The above way of preparation is called "*Hung Shau*", which is the right and best way of preparing the best kind of compact shark's fin. For fins of lower quality or loose fin the semi-final or *(e)* stage of preparation may take one of the following forms:

(1) Cut into small slices the meat of a whole fresh chicken and four ounces of ham (half lean and half fat). Add a glass of wine like sherry and about two cups of water. Then cook them together with the fin in a double saucepan for about three hours or rather until the fin gets quite tender. Serve the whole thing after being salted to taste.

(2) Cook it as in (1). When the fin gets quite tender take it out and cook it with some of the juice in an ordinary pan with fresh crab meat, with or without the "yolk" of the crab, for about 10 minutes over a low fire. Then salt it to taste with pepper and serve the whole thing. The dish, so prepared, should not be in a liquid form, so that not too much of the juice should be used.

2. "BIRD'S NEST".

Its real nature and nutritious properties have been noted. Its preparation is very simple. For one conventional dish use about three ounces, because it is very light. Soak it in lukewarm water for three hours. Pick out all the feathers that are found in it and wash it in cold water gently. When this is done it is clean and ready for cooking. Then cook it in one of the following ways in a *double saucepan*:

(*a*) Stuff it into a whole chicken and cook it with seven cups of water until the chicken becomes quite tender. Then salt it to taste and serve it with the soup and chicken.

(*b*) Cook it with plain but highly tasty chicken broth (enough for 10−12 persons) for two hours over a medium fire. Then salt it to taste and serve the whole thing as soup. As soon as it is dished, sprinkle over it two dessertspoonfuls of finely minced lean ham.

(*c*) Cook it as in (*b*), salt it to taste, and thicken it with a little cornflour. At the same time mince finely an ounce or so of the white meat of a chicken, put this in two tablespoonfuls of cold water, beat up the white of one egg, and mix these well in a liquid form. When the soup is to be served, but not a moment before, pour the mixture into it, stirring well the whole thing. Take care that, before pouring the mix-

ture into the soup, the fire is turned off; otherwise the minced chicken would be overdone and the soup would taste coarse. Lastly, when the soup is actually dished, sprinkle over it two dessertspoonfuls of finely minced lean ham. In taking "Bird's nest" soup made in this way, it is recommended to add a little Chekiang vinegar, if any, which will enhance the taste.

(d) "Bird's nest" can be used as a sweet, in which case it is cooked in plain water for two hours over a medium fire and then sugared to taste. Crystal sugar should be used.

It is interesting to note that "Bird's nest" was known to the Chinese as a delicacy earlier than shark's fin. When the Imperial Palace in Peking was taken over from the last Manchu Monarch, much unused "Bird's nest" was found in the Provision Room with other food materials but practically no shark's fin.

3. FISH LIP.

This is a form of a delicacy known throughout China like shark's fin, so much so that it
sometimes takes the place of the latter in a
banquet. It is the lip part of some kind of fairly
big sea fish, having, apparently, a rich lip, and
is preserved like shark's fin but much easier
to prepare. Its taste is like that of the skirt of
the turtle but more tender, though less rich.
Their nutritious value must be more or less
the same.

Its preparation:

As it is in a dried state with bones attached, it
must first be soaked in cold water for two or
three days until the lip part gets softened. After that, simmer it until all the bones attached
can be easily removed. When this is done,
clean the lip thoroughly and cut it into pieces
of the size of half a playing card. Wash these
pieces once more and put them in a dish. Mix
them with one glass of wine like sherry, some
minced green ginger, and a little pepper, and
leave them in that state for two hours. After
this, wash the pieces thoroughly again and
you will have entirely got rid of the "fishy"
taste of the lip. It is now ready for final preparation.

(a) Cut the meat of a fresh chicken and four
ounces of ham (half lean and half fat) into

pieces and cook them together over a low fire for three hours with two or three cups of water in order to enable them to yield a rich and tasty gravy or juice. In order to save time this should be prepared before the (b) stage.

(b) Put two tablespoonfuls of peanut oil in a frying-pan over a medium fire. As soon as the oil begins to boil, put the lip pieces in, stir them rapidly for a few seconds, and pour two glasses of wine like sherry over them. Then add the chicken, ham, and gravy, with a slice of green ginger and a few pieces of spring onion, and cook the whole mixture over a low fire until the lip pieces get quite (but not too) tender.[1] Spice it to taste with a little pepper. A little soya sauce may be added. Then serve the lip pieces with the gravy only. If the gravy is still a little watery, it may be *slightly* thickened with a little corn starch or flour.

---

1. It takes, perhaps, one hour; for fish lip does not take much time to get tender. That is why the chicken and ham should be cooked first and separately in order to have ready a rich and tasty juice or gravy.

4. TURTLE SKIRT.

This is the soft rim of the shell of the turtle, preserved by being dried in the sun. The nutritious property of the turtle, particularly its skirt, is too well known to require any comment. The dried skirt, when prepared, tastes almost exactly like the fresh one but has more flavour, which has become concentrated through the preservation. Its preparation is exactly like that of the fish lip, *mutatis mutandis*.

Chinese, especially Cantonese, also eat fresh turtle. The best comes from Kwangsi province. It is called *Shan Suey*, "Spirit of the Mountain", because it lives in mountain creeks. It tastes much more delicious than the sea turtle one eats in the West — in the form of "turtle soup".

Its preparation:

(a) After the turtle has been killed and thoroughly cleaned, cut it into pieces of suitable size.

(b) Put them into a *double saucepan* with water enough to make the amount of soup desired. Add two glasses of wine like sherry, half a dozen of fat chicken feet, two pairs of chicken wings, a few dried Chinese "winter" mushrooms (or, as substitute, a few pieces of that dried mushroom called *le bolet* or *la chanterelle comestible*, obtainable at Italian groceries), one dessertspoonful of *Jeou Chii Tzyy* (berries of *lycium chinense*), and half a dozen of the meat of that dried fruit called "Dragon's eye" (both of which are obtainable at a Chinese food store). Then cook it over a medium fire for three or four hours, or a little longer if the chicken feet are not yet tender. Finally, salt it to taste, add a little soya sauce and wine, and serve.

The turtle here is assumed to be of 3-4 lb. gross, so that the ingredients suggested above should vary with its size. However, turtle soup should be rich; therefore, less water should be used than in making the ordinary soup. Three-quarters of a cup allowed for each person would be ample for a Chinese meal, because there may be other soups.

5. ABALONE (BOW YU).

It is produced in Kowloon, Hong Kong, Mexico, some parts of America, Japan, and probably other places too. But the best comes from Japan, because it is more tasty and more tender than others. The Japanese generally eat it raw and sell the dried one to the Chinese, who so relish it as a delicacy that the average man almost forgets that it comes from abroad. It is rich in nutrition, particularly when dried. In 100 grammes it contains:[1]

1 Calories	309
2 Protein	40.6 gm.
3 Fat	1.9 gm.
4 Carbohydrate	28.8 gm.
5 Calcium	170 mg.
6 Phosphorus	442 mg.
7 Iron	7.1 mg. (imputed value)
8 Thiamine	.41 mg.
9 Riboflavin	.37 mg.
10 Niacin value	3.6 mg. (imputed)

(a) Half a pound of this will be sufficient for a dish for 10-12 persons. Clean it thoroughly with warm water and then soak it in *cold* water for four days, changing the water twice a day. After this, clean it again. By this time it is well softened and much enlarged.

(b) Put it in a *double saucepan* (preferably an earthenware one) with about four tablespoonfuls of hot water, some chicken fat or a few slices of fat pork, a dessertspoonful of peanut oil, and a glass of wine like sherry. Then cook it for five hours

---

1. See *Composition of Foods used in Far Eastern Countries, supra.*

over a medium fire. If during the process of cooking it has absorbed all the water and wine and consequently gets dry, add a dessertspoonful of hot water each time.

(c) Then it will be quite tender. Add no salt, unless necessary, or anything else, because the abalone itself is as a rule salty enough. All that remains to be done is to slice it into pieces and serve it with the little juice that is there.

N.B. — After it has been cut into slices, it must not be cooked again, otherwise it will get hardened. Abalone prepared in this way tastes at its best, because its original flavour is preserved 100%. To season the abalone with oyster sauce, as most Cantonese restaurants do, is not the best way of preparing this dish; because the taste of the abalone, which is delicious and unique, would thus be overshadowed by the oyster sauce, which has a predominant taste. Some people, not knowing how to soften the abalone in the right way, would even cook it with a little sodium bicarbonate. This should not be done, for the fine flavour of the abalone would thus be ruined, if not destroyed. The abalone here is assumed to be of good quality. Those of poor quality cannot be made very tender.

6. "Sea Dog" Fish.

This is an amphibious fish which lives in mountain creeks but on a moonlit night would climb up trees to breathe the clear air of the universe. Because of this peculiar habit, some people call it the "Hermit fish". It is black in colour and has no scale, though its skin is unlike that of the eel, which is slippery. If a comparison is needed, it may be said to be rather like an enormous *truite* — the *truite au bleu* one eats on the Continent, though its head is proportionally much bigger. Its usual size is about 3-5 lb. It comes from Kwangsi and Yunnan provinces, but is consumed, perhaps, more in Canton than in its native place; because it is very expensive and the Cantonese, who love good living, are willing to pay a high price for it. It is also the Cantonese cook who can prepare it best. It tastes not entirely like fish. It seems to have some meat taste and makes the most delicious soup, less rich but more delicate in flavour than turtle soup, which is already hard to beat. It is considered most nutritious.

Its preparation:

(a) After it has been cleaned thoroughly, put it in a double saucepan, large enough to hold it as a whole. If you have no such large double saucepan, cut it into three or four pieces horizontally. Then add a few ounces of lean pork and fresh chicken meat, one ounce lean ham, a few "winter" mushrooms (which are required only to bring up the flavour), one small slice of green ginger, one and a half glasses of wine like sherry, and about ten cups of boiling water[1] (which is the right quantity to a fish weighing about 3 lb.).

(b) Cook the whole thing over a medium fire for about two hours, or rather until the fish becomes tender. But do not over-cook it; otherwise, though the soup is very tasty, the fish will be less so. In serving it, add salt to taste and remove the pork, chicken meat, ham, mushroom, and ginger. A *little* soya sauce and pepper may be added.

---

1. The water must be boiling, and the water of the outer saucepan must be boiling too, when the inner saucepan is put in for cooking; otherwise the fish would taste "dull", though the soup may be unaffected.

7. BEAN CURD (TOFU).

It is made of soya bean and used as food by "princes" as well as peasants throughout the country. It contains in 100 grammes the following:[1]

1. Calorie   71
2. Protein   7.0 gm.
3. Fat   4.1 gm.
4. Calcium   100 mg.
5. Phosphorus   95 mg.
6. Iron   1.5 mg.
7. Thiamine   .06 mg.
8. Riboflavin value .05 mg.
9. Niacin   .4 mg.

It is a unique creation of the Chinese in the realm of food. Though one of the cheapest kinds of commodities, it can easily be made into a delicacy and as such may figure in the menu of even a banquet. In a very simple way it can also be made a form of delicious dainty refreshments accessible to people of very limited means. I remember that, the very day on my return to Hong Kong after ten years in England, an old friend told me that, since my departure for Europe, exquisite, dainty refreshments of divers kinds had been created, and that he would be delighted to entertain me to a lunch consisting of these delicacies. To his great surprise, I said, "I would rather have

1. See *Composition of Foods used in Far Eastern Countries, supra.*

a few of the fried *Triangular Tofu* (bean curd) which I enjoyed so much in my school days." He smiled and thought that I was not serious in what I said. To convince him, I wrote down the following verse:

"Ten years' secluded study in the West,
Where choice refreshments sweet
and rich are famed,
Has not subdued my early boyhood zest
For what I used to love
and have just named."

However, this food material is so universal to the Chinese people and so well known that every School of cooking has its special ways of turning it into a delicacy. A few instances may here be indicated. (The quantity is assumed to be for one conventional dish.)

(a) Cut about six pieces (which, individually, are, conventionally, not larger than an ordinary bun) into small pieces of the size of half a domino. Simmer them for 10 seconds and dish them aside. Low-oil-stir-fry some fresh mushrooms cut in slices and dish it aside. Put 3-4 dessertspoonfuls of peanut oil into a frying-pan, large enough to hold these pieces comfortably, over a medium fire. As soon as the oil begins to boil, put the pieces in, and shake them in a circular movement for a few minutes by holding the handle of the pan, so that the hot oil may run over all of them. (The reason for not using a stirring utensil to stir them in the pan is to avoid breaking any of them.) Then pour over them 2-3 tablespoonfuls of oyster sauce, lower the fire, and shake them in the same way until the oyster sauce has permeated them thoroughly. Then add the mushroom slices, stir the whole thing once more, and

serve. No salt but pepper may be added, because the oyster sauce is salty enough.

(b) Cut about five pieces into cubes of the
size of a dice, put them in a sieve, and pour
over them a quart of very hot water (or put
them in a frying-basket and clip them for 10
seconds into boiling water). When the water
has run through the sieve, put three dessertspoonfuls of peanut oil in a frying-pan over a
medium fire. As soon as the oil begins to boil,
put in fresh shrimps (cut into the size of the
cubes and about one-third in quantity in proportion to the latter). Stir the shrimps rapidly
for 10 seconds and add the cubes with a little
spring onion finely cut up. Raise the fire a bit
and stir the whole thing, so that the shrimps
and the cubes may mix even. At the same time
add some green peas and some fresh mushroom cut in cubes, both of which have been
cooked separately, half a glass of wine like
sherry, a dessertspoonful of soya sauce, salt to
taste, and a pinch of pepper. Turn the fire off,
stir the whole thing once more, and serve.

(c) Cut about four pieces into squares of
about one inch in size and two-tenths of an
inch in thickness. Simmer them for 30 seconds
and then cook them for one hour over a low
fire with pork and chicken broth salted to taste,
a little spice, and soya sauce. After this put a
piece of ham over each of them, dip them into
well-beaten eggs *slightly* thickened with flour,

and have them deep-fried until they get brown.

(d) Cut each piece into two of triangular shape. Make a fairly large hole in the middle on the side that has been cut and stuff it with minced shrimp and fish meat, well seasoned with finely cut spring onion, soya sauce, pepper, and, if possible, bits of fried peanut, and then have it fried in deep oil until it gets brown. This can be served as refreshments.

(e) Bean curd cooked with fish is also delicious. Cut it into pieces as in (a). Put two tablespoonfuls of peanut oil in a frying-pan and have the fish fried in whole over a low fire, until its two sides have got brown. Pour over it one glass of wine like sherry, mixed with a little minced green ginger, add a tablespoonful of soya sauce, some spring onion, salt to taste, and one cup of water (which may be added, when it has been absorbed). Cook it thus for 15 minutes, add bean curd, and let the whole thing be cooked together until the fish is well done.

8. Bean Sprouts.

There are two kinds: those of the soya bean and those of the Mung bean, popularly called "green peas". Both must be the most marvellous vegetables known to the world; for they can grow in a few days and in all times of the year. They are delicious as well as rich in vitamin C. In 100 grammes they respectively contain:[1]

	Soya Bean Sprouts	Mung Bean Sprouts
1. Calorie	46	23
2. Protein	6.2 gm.	2.9 gm.
3. Fat	1.4 gm.	.2 gm.
4. Carbohydrate	5.3 gm.	4.1 gm.
5. Calcium	48 mg.	29 gm.
6. Phosphorus	67 mg.	59 gm.
7. Iron	1.0 mg.	0.8 gm.
8. Vitamin A value	180 I.U.	10 I.U.
9. Thiamine	.23 mg.	.07 mg.
10. Riboflavin	.20 mg.	.09 mg.
11. Niacin value	.8 mg.	.5 mg.
12. Ascorbic Acid	13 mg.	15 mg.

The latter is very easy to grow. To make 2 lb. of sprouts you need only about one cup of mung bean: Soak it in cold water for 2-3 days. As soon as its shell begins to break and a little sprout reveals itself, put it into a tub, or an earthenware pot, of suitable size, with a hole in the bottom, which should be covered up in such a way that no water would remain and no bean would slip through. Cover the tub or the pot with a damp cloth, put it in a dark place with a temperature of 70-75 degrees, and water it six or seven times a day. Thus ev-

---

1. See *Composition of Foods used in Far Eastern Countries, supra.*

ery day you will see the sprouts shoot up and in less than a week you will have a lovely crop of them. When they are nice and "plump", empty them into a tray and keep them in a cool place; they must not be allowed to over-grow. Before using them for cooking, the root end of each sprout should be picked off.

The proper way of cooking bean sprouts of either kind is *Chow* (low-oil-quick-stir-frying). They can be cooked simply by themselves or with celery or with meat or poultry, of which all, in each case, should be cut into slices more or less equivalent in size to the sprouts. But they must not be over-done; otherwise their inherent delicate taste and the vitamins they contain will be ruined. The test is that they should taste crisp when cooked. They can also be used as salad.

9. Preserved Duck's Egg.

Westerners, though they may love Chinese food in general, often hesitate to eat this, owing to its changed colour, thinking that it might have been dug up from some tomb of the *Tang* or *Sung* dynasty! Personally, I know one Westerner who loves it. He is a Portuguese duke. However, these eggs are in fact no more than 50 days old, if preserved in the modern way, or 100 days old if preserved in the old way. They are preserved by a solution of salt, lime, and soda or potash, in water according to modern methods, or by a clayey paste made up of the same composition according to the old. The use of lime and soda accounts for the change of colour of the egg. The best of these eggs are made in Peking, where they are preserved in such a way that they contain five distinct colours, one after another. How this is achieved is a secret, but the principle of preservation is the same. In either case the taste of the egg, though a little "acquired", is delicious and makes a very good *hors d'œuvre* for *apéritif*. Such eggs are particularly good for those who suffer from hyperacidity and stomach ulcers; because they have, through the process of preservation, been alkalinized and can thus act as antidote to that ailment besides their own nutritional value. It is delicious when eaten with pickled ginger or soya sauce with a little vinegar or Worcester sauce or even plain. A thesis on the preserved egg was written about the time of World War I by a young Chinese lady for her postgraduate degree in an American University.

10. BEAR'S PAW.

It may seem paradoxical that the list of special delicacies should be closed with this, which must be the earliest delicacy known to the Chinese; for even Mencius, the great philosopher of pre-Christian era who lived about 100 years after Confucius, said: "Fish is what I like, so are bear's paws; but, if I cannot have both, I will forgo the fish and choose the bear's paws. Similarly, I love life and I also love righteousness; but if I cannot have both, I will forgo life and choose righteousness."[1] The reason for reserving it to the last is because it is fast becoming a delicacy of only historical interest; for its supply is very limited and restaurants in these days often use, as its substitute, buffalo's feet, which, if well prepared, taste rather like bear's paw, and of which the identity can never be discovered by those who have not tasted the latter before or, though they may have done so, are no connoisseurs. In fact, it is chiefly a delicacy of the North and, generally speaking, can be properly prepared only by cooks of the Shantung or Honan Schools. The taste of bear's paw is unique. The nearest comparison is that it is like the fat part of the best ham, or rather much better, for it has not the greasiness of the latter. It is so smooth and delicious that it simply melts in one's mouth. It must be highly rich in nutritious properties.

Its preparation as told:

The paw is wrapped in mud (clean mud of course) and then baked in the oven. When the mud becomes firm like clay, it is taken out and, when it is cool, the mud is torn off. This will automatically bring the hairy skin off the paw, and you will thus get the meat fit for food.

---

1. *Mencius*, Bk. VI, Pt. I, Ch. 10, Sec. 1.

The next process is to simmer it to get it softened, changing the water frequently in order to get rid of its gamey smell and taste.

When it has become softened and "tasteless", a condition that is essential, then cook it until it is tender, over a simmering fire with chicken meat, lean ham, and wine like sherry, with water just enough to enable the ingredients to yield a rich and thick gravy. When served, it should be cut in slices like ham.

CHAPTER NINE

Hints on Cooking

AS COOKING is partly an art and partly a science, as already discussed, there must be certain underlying principles, a firm grasp of which is essential to any attempt to do good cooking. A person who aspires to be an accomplished carpenter does not merely learn how to make a chair or table, but first learns the principles of carpentry. Similarly, one who aspires to be a good speaker does not merely commit to memory set speeches but first studies the principles of public speaking. In painting or calligraphy one even goes further. Though at first one imitates the great masters, afterwards one tries to break away from them in order to develop one's own originality. To a certain extent it is the same with cooking. An original "touch" is always refreshing and makes a special appeal to the palate. In a previous chapter a distinction has been drawn between "dishes by the gourmet" and those by the professional. It is always the former that bear "touches" of originality, though the latter can be assured of their "virtue" of uniformity. Forsooth, anyone who follows a cookery book can make some dishes of some sort; but, unless he has a grasp of the principles, he cannot go beyond his limited sphere or improve any recipe he has copied. Still less can he "cure" any dish that has gone wrong, or create any dish of his own. If the instructions given in the cookery book happen to be wrong, he repeats the mistakes. There are, for instance, cookery books which suggest the use of sodium bicarbonate as a means of softening abalone or shark's fin—a device which, if followed, would ruin, if not destroy, at least part, if not the whole, of the inherent taste of the material. Even when the instructions are correct, they cannot be followed blindly. In cooking dishes, unlike in making pastries and the like, which may be comparatively more exact in prescription, such detailed instructions as to the *time* that is necessary, or the amount of *oil* or *water* or the like to be used, are only relative. They serve merely as guidance. One must therefore use one's own judgment in all cases. Above all, however good a recipe may be, there is always room for improvement. Regard, therefore, every performance as an experiment and you will be on the road to the kingdom of good cooking.

With the above observation a few hints may now be discussed. Some of them have already been given in the chapter on "What is Good Cooking?" They will not be repeated here, but it is necessary to recall the definition of good cooking therein given:

> "The employment of the process of culinary art in producing what is appetizing to the eye, the nose, and the palate, and agreeable to the stomach. . . . In particular, the food concerned is cooked to the right point (as a rule neither underdone nor overdone); though rich, as the case may be, but not too rich and never greasy; tender, when it should be ten-

der; crisp, when it should be crisp; and undominated by the taste of anything added to or cooked with it (such as sauce or accessories of any kind) unless this is purposely intended (such as in making curry and the like) but preserving in full, or to the largest extent possible, its original flavour, whether it is meat, sea food, or vegetable."

The various conditions embodied in the definition require elucidation, which, when given, will also supply some hints on cooking.

(1) *Cooked to the right point.*

A thing "underdone" here does not necessarily mean that it is partly raw, as in roast beef. Certain dishes, such as stews and the like, require to be well done. To be not so well done is "underdone", i.e. not cooked to the right point. Similarly, "overdone" does not necessarily mean that the thing has been cooked to the point that it has been somewhat ruined or spoiled. It simply means that it has been cooked beyond the point at which it would taste at its best—a finesse that can be appreciated only by the gourmet. For instance, when a delicate fish, such as trout, is cooked by steaming, even a minute too long would make the fish taste "hard". When cooked just to the right point, it tastes not only tender but also "crisp", which is the highest mark of freshness and the summit of taste in sea food of all kinds.

If fish is cooked not by steaming but with some ingredients, such as bean curd, fresh or dried, aubergine (egg plant), etc., a little "overdoing" makes little difference. It is even advisable to err on the right side, if one is timid.

(2) *Though rich – but not too rich and never greasy.*

Certain dishes, such as roast duck, turtle, shark's fin in *Hung Shau* style, some kinds of stew, and the like, should be rich. Indeed, they should look rich as well as taste rich. Yet there is a limit. Anything that is overflowed with oil or fat, however tasty it may be, is apt to stun one's appetite. "Rich" has also a meaning in another sense, i.e. highly tasty, and there can be such a thing as "over-tasty". Taste, like aroma in perfume, has its maximum, intended by nature. When this maximum is exceeded, it ceases to be "tasty" and may become even repulsive to the palate. For instance, assuming that one chicken is sufficient to make a very tasty soup for, say six persons, then if you use two or even three for making the same amount of soup, you will be making not proper chicken broth but chicken essence, which, like any other essence, cannot be taken as such. This principle applies not only to soup but also to other dishes or cookings *mutatis mutandis*. When a thing is greasy, it is, of course, wrong. All grease should always be removed.

(3) *Tender, when it should be tender; crisp, when it should be crisp.*

Dishes such as stews, Chinese *Hung Shau*, and the like, should be tender. In these, a little "overdone" will not hurt. If you are "timid", it is better to err on the right side; for it is essential that the principal thing should be permeated by the juice in which it is cooked. To be not tender enough in this kind of cooking is "underdone", or rather not cooked to the right point.

Certain things (or dishes) should taste "crisp". This applies to all things deep-fried, to all low-oil-quick-stir-frying (*Chow*) dishes, and to certain steamed dishes, such as fish, minced pork with minced water-chestnut, etc. When that crispness is not attained or is lost, it is a failure.

(4) *Unpredominated by the taste of anything added to or cooked with the food concerned (such as sauce or accessories of any kind) unless this is purposely intended (such as in making curry and the like), but preserving in full, or to the largest extent, etc.*

Anything that is good for food has its own original taste endowed by nature, whether it is meat, poultry, sea food, or vegetable, though, in some cases, this original flavour has to be brought out in its best condition by some device in the use of the right accompanying ingredients. For instance, the meat of a duck or chicken has its own taste distinct from that of any other species of the "bird" family; so does one form of sea food as regards others. This being so, it is only good sense that this distinct taste, if good, should, as a rule, be preserved as far as possible. It would, therefore, be bad cooking to prepare anything in such a way as to cause it to lose its original taste or to transform it into something else or to over-encumber it with things, having a strong taste of their own, like putting paint and powder on the faces of angels. Allowance is, of course, made for those cases, very popular in Chinese cooking, where it is intended to create a "mixed" taste, like the *Bouillabaisse* of Provence, or a "community" of taste like the Danish *Lobescobes*, of which the late Danish King Christian X was reputed to be very fond. For this reason, the way in which the "Pressed duck", for which the restaurant *Tour d'Argent*, in Paris, is famous, does not seem to be the best way of cooking a duck. First of all, the duck is partly cooked at the preliminary stage and then cooked again over a spirit lamp, a process like smoking a cigar which has been half-smoked but left over and then lit again. Secondly, nearly all parts of the duck except the breast are ground into juice for cooking the latter in the second process, in order, no doubt, to add more taste to it. Admittedly, the breast of the duck, thus treated, is made very tasty, because it incorporates the taste of almost the whole duck. But such device is rather like adding the fine beard of a man to his fine moustache in order to make the moustache look even finer. Nature has her secret that the breast of the duck (or, for that matter, any other part of the bird) is endowed with all the sweetness that properly belongs to it. If you think, by adding to it the taste of the rest of the duck, you will "improve" nature, you are in fact transforming it. In other words, by such a process, you do not improve nature but change nature. Thus the "Pressed duck", though very tasty as a dish, does not taste like duck at all. To a certain extent this applies to that famous dish *Pompano en Papillotte*, where plenty of crab meat, diced cooked shrimp, and fish stock are used in addition to flavouring ingredients. If the pompano is so prized as it is, to encumber it with such common sea food as crab meat, shrimp, and fish stock is rather like painting an angel with a gold chain or diamond ring. In this light there is much to be said for the English or American way of cooking roast beef or grilled steak or chop, simple (in the sense of simplicity) though it

is; because it conforms to nature, without attempting to "improve" it. In fact, it is the ideal way, though there may be room for improvement in the choice of the fire used. For instance, in some districts in Canton, charcoal of the pine tree is used for roasting meat (e.g. pigs) or poultry, with the result that an unusually delicious flavour is attained. Apropos of beef steak, though French cooking is generally excellent, one may venture the opinion that, if a "plebiscite" were held, the majority would vote for the English or American beef steak rather than for the French *Châteaubriand*. The latter is, after all, only a form of beef steak — a very choice one, no doubt — but its inner part is almost cold and practically raw, thus giving it an acquired taste. To put two pats of butter over a beef steak as restaurants in Paris often do is also like painting the lily. To many, the steak would taste better *qua* steak without this rich addition.

From the above discussion it may be formulated that simplicity is a secret in the art of cooking, but how to attain excellence through simplicity is the true essence of art. It also follows that it is not a very good form of cooking, though it may produce something very appetizing:

(*a*) To use too often or too much tomato or tomato sauce with or without cheese as in some Western cuisines.
(*b*) To make most, if not all, dishes hot as in some Eastern cuisines or in some Chinese provincial cooking.
(*c*) To use too often or too much garlic as some people are fond of doing.
(*d*) To use too much or in everything the soya sauce as in some Chinese provincial cookings.

The soya sauce is, indeed, a wonderful invention of the Chinese as a condiment or as a substitute for salt at the table; because it does enhance the taste of food in general, if used discriminately. I have been told by a friend that an American colleague of his is so fond of it that he uses it like beef essence and drinks a cup of this mixture—that is, hot water and soya sauce, every morning. I myself have also sometimes noticed that American people eating Chinese food would shower soya sauce over it. This is, of course, a display of excessive love for the soya sauce. However, the very fact that it is very tasty in itself makes it easily noticeable. If used in an "overdose", it will drown or modify the original flavour of the food concerned, especially where the flavour is a delicate one. And if used in everything, it will make every dish taste almost the same to an alien, or the trained, palate. Moreover, if certain tasty ingredients are used to cook with the food concerned, they will yield a sauce of their own, which should not be tampered with by another sauce having a sharp taste.

(e) To use sugar to "enhance" taste.

Certain dishes, like Chinese *Hung Shau* meat or anything cooked with "Sweet and Sour" sauce, require, of course, the use of sugar, apart from some other cookings where just a pinch of sugar may be allowed. But to use it indiscriminately in order to "enhance" taste, as some people are inclined to do, would be like adding sugar to human milk, as if it were not made sweet enough by Nature. Anything that is good for food and properly prepared as such has a sweetness of its own like "mother's milk", which Nature in her mysterious and unfathomable way has made sweet enough for the child. Any sweet substance, such as sugar, added to it would only tamper with Nature and create a "sweetness" of an entirely different kind. For this reason in the preparation of certain kinds of soup, which may be enhanced in flavour by some sweet taste imparted to it, the Canton School uses not sugar but certain herbs or dried fruits of a sweet nature, such as berries of *lycium chinense*, unsweetened dates, or "Dragon's Eye", a fruit that grows in South China. The result is very different.

Apropos of the use of sugar, the worst is the use, in good cooking, of a certain chemical compound known as sodium glutamate, quite in vogue these days. Though harmless, it has no nutritious value. It creates no taste, as believed it would, but only a semblance of taste like saccharin as a substitute for sugar. A person who tastes it the first time may be deceived; but after a few times he will always find it there — a "mechanical" taste intolerable to the gourmet.

Incidental to the above discussion there are a few other hints that may be noted:

1. PRINCIPAL AND ACCESSORY.

In preparing any dish, if a certain thing is, as generally in Chinese cooking, cooked with certain ingredients, the latter are accessories, and the question arises, what and how much of the latter should be used? The first part of the question requires discretion, experience, and a knowledge of things that can be used as a substitute when the particular thing needed is unobtainable. In general the ingredients used should fit in with the nature of the principal and be able to enhance, or benefit by, the taste of the latter. As instances of substitutes, kohlrabi, asparagus tips, broccoli, and French beans, if cut and used in the right way, may, as a "second best" or even as a change, take the place of bamboo shoots, bean sprouts, and the like. As regards proportion, particularly in Chinese cooking, where meat is often cut in slices or cubes and cooked with vegetables or other ingredients cut more or less in the same way, the answer is: if meat is the principal, the accessory should not be more than two-fifths in proportion; conversely, the accessory should not be more than one-quarter. The reason is, in the former the accessory is meant to be a combination; in the latter it is used only to give the principal a flavour.

2. "RULE OF SYMMETRY".

In Chinese cooking, accessory ingredients forming part of the dish and cooked in the form of a "Mixture" should, as far as possible, be cut to the same size as the principal, so that they may mix well and benefit one another, apart from presenting thus a harmonious appearance. It would look incongruous if meat

cut in cubes were cooked with accessory ingredients cut in slices.

3. "Principle of Parts".

The principle is actually applied universally without being recognized as such. For instance, different parts of a sheep or an ox are sold separately and used for different purposes, such as for chop or steak, for roasting, for stew, for soup, etc. This is largely due to the fact that one would seldom buy a whole sheep and still less a whole ox. In consequence, the animal has to be sold in parts, and this led to the discovery that, in fact, different parts have their own merits and can be best used for different purposes according to their natural composition. But the application of this principle to smaller animals like poultry, apart from fish of large size, is comparatively a recent phenomenon in some Western countries. In China, however, this principle has been recognized almost since the dawn of the Chinese cuisine. Therefore, one can in a well-provided market buy separately any part of the chicken, duck, or goose, or only the giblets or the feet or the tongues of ducks. Like the "Crêtes de Coq", as used in the French cuisine, all the latter can be made a delicacy. Dining informally in a Chinese restaurant one may order "chicken cooked in three ways" or "fish cooked in two or four ways", thus getting three dishes from one chicken and two or four dishes from one fish—all are exquisitely done and delicious.

4. Use Pure Fat.

Fat to cooking is like water to tea or coffee. If not pure, it will spoil the whole thing. Therefore, as a rule use peanut oil, which has a neutral taste. Sometimes, lard made actually from pig's fat may be used but not so-called lard bought at the shop, which may have been made from any fat and in some cases has a repulsive taste, reminding one of the story told by Sam Weller about the sausage! Western cuisines use butter of course, which, though excellent and pure, has no place in Chinese cooking, and, as it has a strong flavour of its own, gives the thing it cooks with a "National" taste in the sense discussed in a former chapter.

5. "Secrets" in the Use of Condiments.

As cooking is largely an art, any material used only for enhancing the flavour, such as garlic, onion, spice, ginger, pepper, or the like should be used in such a quantity and way as would not make it betray itself. To leave the diner in doubt as to what has been used is a success. Hence, garlic or ginger is often used only to rub the pan with before the actual cooking begins or only a pinch of it is used. Sometimes, just one dried mushroom is used in making soup in order to give it a touch of undiscoverable flavour. However, green ginger and spring onion are very effective ingredients in counteracting the "fishy" smell of the fish.

6. "SECRETS" IN STEAMING FISH

(Knowledge of using the ingredients is assumed).

Cooking by steaming is one of, if not the best, means of cooking fresh fish, for it preserves the delicate taste of the fish 100%. It is for this reason that on the Continent live trout are generally cooked *au bleu*; for it is only in this way that one can taste in full the freshness and delicate flavour of the fish. This form of cooking is very generally used in the Chinese cuisine, particularly in home cooking. It is rather remarkable that it is hardly, if ever, employed in Western cuisines. However, as it is a form of swift cooking, all the means available to quicken the process should be utilized. Thus:

(I) The water in the steaming utensil should be of such a quantity as capable of producing a large volume of steam and must be actually boiling before the fish held by the plate is put in.

(II) The plate destined to hold the fish should first be heated in the steaming utensil before the fish is put on it with all the accompanying ingredients.

(III) As soon as the fish has been put in, cover the utensil and raise the fire to the maximum point.

(IV) Serve the fish when it is about 99%[1] cooked and without changing the plate, which, if not presentable, may be put on a more presentable one, but should not be changed if the fish is to be tasted at its best.

---

1. Originally this figure was written as 99.7%, meaning, of course, less than 100%, but a friend of mine, learned in science, "challenged" me on this figure, asking me how to measure it. My answer was that it must not be taken too literally, just as trains are often scheduled to be due at 7.11 instead of 7.10 or 3.49 instead of 3.50. We both laughed, but in deference to his scientific exactitude, I have now made it read 99%.

The whole idea of the process indicated is to get the fish cooked by an overwhelming heat in a minimum of time, so as to preserve in full the freshness and delicate flavour of the fish (or for that matter, any other form of sea food, such as crabs). If the water is not actually boiling when the fish is put in, this would be equivalent to leaving it in a warm place until the water reaches the boiling point. This interval, short though it may be, has the effect of more or less ruining the fresh and delicate taste of the fish. For this reason even the plate for holding the fish should he heated first before the fish is transferred to it—a hint that may well be regarded as a "secret", because this is seldom, if ever, done. The fish should be served when it is about 99% cooked; because in that hot state when the plate is lifted from the steaming utensil, the process of cooking still continues, so that the fish will automatically become 100% cooked when it reaches the dining-table. It is for this reason that the plate should not be changed.

7. "THE THREE STAGES".

Meat, cut in slices in making soup with other flavouring ingredients, as the Chinese often do, varies in taste and in effect according to the length of time for which it is cooked:

(I) When the meat slices are just cooked

(which would mean about 99% cooked when served, because the process of cooking continues, as already discussed) the soup is tasty and the meat also tender.

(II) When the meat slices are cooked beyond (I) stage — assuming, of course, that the quantity is the same as in (I) — the soup is less tasty and the meat no longer tender.

(III) When the slices are cooked to the tender point through continued boiling, the soup may be tasty but the meat is hardly eatable.

"THE TWO WAYS".

When poultry is cooked in whole to be eaten with the soup resulting from it, as is often done in Chinese cooking, there are two ways:

(I) If more importance is attached to the soup, use cold water at the beginning.

(II) If more importance is attached to the "bird", use boiling water at the beginning.

The above rules apply to large pieces of meat cooked in the same way.

8. HOW TO DO "LOW-OIL-QUICK-STIR-FRYING" (CHOW) DISHES.

(a) In the case of meat, use fillet without any fat; in the case of poultry, use the breast part without the skin.

(b) Cut it in cross vein into slices, as desired.

(c) Cut the accessories (which should be suitable vegetables, such as bamboo shoot, kohlrabi, the stem of broccoli, asparagus tips, onion, fresh mushroom, and the like) into sizes according to the "Rule of symmetry".

(d) If the principal is meat, mix the slices with a little flour in a little water and soya sauce (or, as a substitute, Vesop or Maggi) or oyster sauce (which is the best for this purpose). If the principal is chicken, first soak the slices for a few minutes in a small bowl of cold water with a little salt, so as to harden them a little and prevent them from sticking together when cooked. No sauce of any kind should be used, because that would darken the colour, but the slices may, after they have been taken out of the salted water, be mixed with a little flour as in the case of meat.

(e) Mince a slice of green ginger and mix it with one dessertspoonful of wine like sherry. After the minced ginger has set, pour the wine into a glass and have it ready for the final process.

(f) Put 2-3 dessertspoonfuls (which are only relative) of peanut oil in a frying-pan. When the oil begins to boil, throw the accessories in, turn the fire to the medium height, and stir them all the time until they are cooked. During this process water and oil in small quantity may be added from time to time to prevent the ingredients from getting too dry or being burnt. Salt them to taste and dish them aside. If the accessories are green vegetables, such as French beans or broccoli (but not bamboo shoot, asparagus tips, or mushroom), put them first in boiling water for one minute or so and then immediately cool them with icy water, so as to have them softened and their greenness preserved as well as to facilitate their cooking in the "low-oil-quick-stir-frying" process.

(g) Now comes the final performance. Put 2-3 dessert-spoonfuls (which are only relative) of peanut oil in a *clean* pan over a low fire and rub the pan all over with a piece of garlic. When the oil begins to boil, raise the fire to the maximum point and throw the principal in. With a utensil like a pancake turner, *press it hard against the pan* to make direct contact. At the same time stir it swiftly, so that it may thus be cooked evenly. When it is about 80% cooked, throw the accessories in and stir the mixture thoroughly. At the same time cover the mixture, for a few seconds, with the plate on which the mixture is to be dished, so that it may "get a taste" of the mixture, as it were (which is a "secret" in getting what is called "*Walk He*" mentioned in a previous chapter). When the principal is cooked about 90%, pour the wine in (along the side of the pan, not over the mixture) and stir the mixture thoroughly for the last time. Serve it when cooked about 97%, because the "process of cooking" continues in that hot state. No salt need be added, because everything has already been salted to taste in the preliminary stage.

In this form of cooking there should be practically no juice. If there is plenty of juice, such juice would be stewing the mixture and mar the process of "low-oil-quick-stir-frying". Therefore, no water should, but more oil may, be added during the process, when the mixture gets too dry. If necessary, the fire may be turned low and the pan covered for a few seconds so that the steam thus engendered may moisten the mixture.

9. WHEN FRUITS AND VEGETABLES ARE AT THEIR BEST.

Bacon says, "Justice is sweetest when it is freshest." Generally speaking, vegetables and fruits are sweetest when they are cheapest, because they are in season. It is, of course, fashionable to eat what is not in season; but this does not conform to the law of nature and is to miss what is really best.

10. A "POSTSCRIPT" AND A FEW SIMPLE BUT SPECIAL RECIPES FOR LOVERS OF CHINESE FOOD

Even the best cooking may be marred by a little oversight; for instance, meat or poultry may have been cut on a chopping-board[1] on which fish has been cut and which has not been thoroughly cleaned. Provide your kitchen with three chopping-boards — one for meat, onc for vegetables, and one for fish — and several spare clean dish-cloths always ready for use.

1. *"Washington Omelette"*.

This is so named because it was created in 1922 during the Washington Conference. Its

---

1. The Chinese "chopping-board" is about one foot in diameter and three inches in thickness and is made of wood from the trunk of some special tree.

ingredients and preparation:

2 dozen oysters, minced with chopping-knives.
3 oz. fat pork, minced with chopping-knives.
6 Cantonese preserved olives, called "Lam Sze", or as substitute stoned Spanish olives, cut up finely.
1 piece of spring onion, cut up finely.
7-8 eggs well beaten up.
2 teaspoonfuls of soya sauce (or Vesop or Maggi).
2 teaspoonfuls of peanut oil.

Mix the above ingredients well and salt to taste. Add a little
water as in making custard, taking into consideration the water content of the oysters. If possible, add six cooked water
chestnuts and an ounce of shrimps, all finely cut up. Then put
the mixture in a flat plate with a turned-up edge and have it
steamed or baked in an oven, like cooking custard.

2. "*No. 8*" (which is really Chop Suey; but this is a special
recipe).

It is a dish composed of various kinds of vegetables cut, if possible, to the size of a domino, cooked with the white meat of
chicken or lean pork, cut in slices. The essential vegetables are
onion, cabbage, mushroom, celery, bean sprouts, water chestnut, and bamboo shoot. If bean sprouts and bamboo shoot
are not available, French beans, asparagus tips, and the stems
of broccoli may be used as substitutes. The various kinds of
vegetables should be more or less in equal proportion and the
meat should be about one-fourth or one-fifth of the vegetables
combined. Cabbage and French beans, because they take longer time to cook than the other vegetables, should be first put

in *boiling* water and boiled for 3-4 minutes and then cooled in cold water, so that they may be softened and their greenness preserved. Now how to cook:

(The amount of oil indicated hereafter is only relative and the oil mentioned is peanut oil).

(a) Put three dessertspoonfuls of oil in a pan over a medium fire. As soon as it begins to boil, put one peeled tomato in, press it with a cooking-spoon, and add a little water in order to make juice.

(b) As soon as the tomato has yielded the juice as desired, put in the onion first, then the cabbage (and French beans, if used), then the mushroom, water chestnut, and bamboo shoot, and lastly the celery and the bean sprouts. The latter are put in last, because they require less time to cook. While these things are put in one after another, they should be stirred all the time, and, if they get dry, a little oil and water should be added from time to time; but there should not he too much juice. During this process the pan may be covered for a few seconds, in order that some steam may thus be engendered so as to prevent the mixture from getting dry.

(c) As soon as this vegetarian mixture is cooked, add the meat (chicken or pork) slices in with one dessertspoonful of soya sauce and

salt to taste. Stir the whole mixture until the meat is about 95% cooked, when it should be served.

N.B. — The meat slices may first be mixed with a little flour in a little water with a teaspoonful of soya sauce.

3. *"Crystal" Chicken.*

This is a very popular Cantonese dish and the following way of cooking is original, making the chicken taste most tender and preserving its inherent flavour 100%. It is so called because of a pun, meaning "cooked through being soaked in boiling water". The chicken must be very fresh and tender. If not, it will not be fit for this form of cooking. Now, how to cook:

(*a*) Use the chicken whole and insert into it two or three metal spoons for conducting heat.

(*b*) Use a saucepan large enough to hold sufficient water to cover the whole chicken. Have the latter boiled to the bubbling point and add a slice of green ginger and a piece of spring onion or a few slices of onion, which are intended to counteract the oily taste of the skin of the chicken.

(*c*) While the water is boiling, put the chicken in. As the chicken is cold, the water will then cease to boil. Therefore, bring the water up to the bubbling point again. About 30 seconds after the water has reached this point turn the fire off and cover the saucepan. Leave the chicken in the water until the latter gets cold (about three hours), and the chicken will be just 100% cooked without losing any of its flavour, inasmuch as the water in which it is cooked is practically tasteless.

The chicken should not be cut up for serving until it is quite cold. The best sauce for it is soya sauce mixed with cooked peanut oil and finely cut spring onion. But it can be eaten with any other sauce or just with salt and pepper. Cantonese would mix the salt with a little cooked peanut oil, minced raw ginger, and finely cut spring onion.

4. *"Fu Yung" Crab.*

This is a popular dish for Europeans and Americans and can be easily prepared:

(*a*) Have mushroom, onion, French beans, and bamboo shoot (or the stems of broccoli or asparagus tips as substitute) in suitable quantity more or less equal in proportion as accessories and have them cut in slices. The French beans should be first softened in boiling water. The crab meat being the principal should be in substantial quantity.

(*b*) Put 2-3 dessertspoonfuls of oil in a frying-pan over a medium fire. When the oil begins to boil, put the onion and French beans in and stir them well. Then add bamboo shoot or its substitute. When all of them are nearly cooked, add the mushroom, which is put in last, because it takes less time to cook than the others. Stir the mixture well and salt it to taste in addition to a little soya sauce. As soon as all are cooked, put in the crab meat and stir the whole thing evenly, so that all the ingredients may mix well. As the crab meat is generally already cooked, it should not be cooked too long a second time. Therefore, the whole thing may be dished aside after two or three stirs.

(c) Beat up a few eggs, enough to make some sort of an om-elette with the mixture described in *(b)*, add it in, and stir the whole thing evenly. Before heating up the eggs, add cooked oil (one teaspoonful to every two eggs).

(d) Put three dessertspoonfuls of oil in a clean frying-pan over a medium fire. As soon as the oil begins to boil, raise the fire and throw the whole thing in, spreading it wide over the pan, and stir it rapidly with a utensil like a pancake turner or a big spoon, as in cooking scrambled egg. As soon as the egg is about 98% cooked (because the process of cooking still continues), dish it in a hot plate and serve.

5. *"Most Precious Rice"*.

This is generally known as *Chow Fan*, well liked by Western-ers and indeed by all. The only question is how it may be best prepared. It is called "Most Precious" because it consists of various tasty ingredients besides rice: mushroom, shrimp (or crab meat), green peas, bamboo shoot (or French beans), chicken meat (or pork), spring onion, egg, and lean ham. How to cook:

(a) All the ingredients, except the rice and the egg, should be cut to the size of a small pea, and except the spring onion, which is used only for flavouring and therefore should be in small quantity, their proportion should be more or less the same.

(b) The rice should be cooked and cold; its proportion to

the ingredients should be about ten to one.

(c) The eggs should be beaten up with a little soya sauce (or Vesop or Maggi as a substitute). How many eggs should be used depends on the quantity of rice. One egg to two rice-bowls of rice, however, is sufficient.

(d) Cook in a frying-pan with oil the vegetarian ingredients mentioned in *(a)* in the same way as in *(b)* in cooking the ingredients for the *Fu Yung* crab. When these ingredients are nearly cooked, add the meat, shrimp or crab meat, ham, and spring onion. These are added last, because they do not take much time to cook. As soon as all are cooked add salt to taste and dish the whole thing aside.

(e) Put a few spoonfuls of oil in a frying-pan over a medium fire. As soon as the oil begins to boil, put the rice in and stir it thoroughly and evenly. During this process, if it gets too dry, a little oil and water may be added from time to time. When it becomes separate and quite hot, throw the ingredients in and stir the whole thing rapidly so as to get it well mixed. Then pour the liquid eggs over the whole mixture, raise the fire, and stir it again rapidly until the eggs have mixed it evenly and get fairly dry. Then serve.

CHAPTER TEN

A Talk on Chinese Wine

THAT a good dinner should be accompanied with good wine is a statement that would hardly be contested, except, perhaps, by those who, for reason of religion or health or by habit, are or have become teetotallers. This is so true that in certain countries, the older cultural institutions, whose intellectual giants dine sumptuously at regular intervals of the year, have very fine cellars. And this must also be my justification for including in this book a talk on wine, particularly Chinese wine, which is still hardly known by the world.

In China wine is served at all feasts, whether the occasion is a wedding or a funeral. Whether it is drunk by the guests or not is another matter. It seems that wine simply forms part and parcel of a feast, which in Chinese is called *yen* (or *yin* in Cantonese), meaning, according to the dictionary, "entertaining guests with wine and food". Without it, a meal, however elaborate, loses, it seems, that dignity. With it, a meal, though modest, rises to the level of entertainment. To illustrate this, there can be no better instance than the following extracts from a classical poem, which may be translated as:

"Who knew, indeed, full twenty years before
I would ascend thy hall today once more?
When last we parted, thou hadst not a spouse.
A group of children now adorn thy house,

They gladly come to hail their father's guest,
And ask his native home with welcome zest.
Though hardly can I speak a word of mine,
  Boys and girls engage in pouring wine.
Spring greens are cut amidst nocturnal rain
For a new-cooked meal with *yellow grain*."[1]

Here the meal, as described, is simple indeed; but, with wine, it at once assumes the form of an entertainment. However, in all instances of sacrificial offerings, whether to God or to ancestors, wine forms a part. But it must not be thought from all this that the Chinese are a "drinking nation". They are by nature and habit just the opposite; for the people in general rarely drink, if ever, and do not care for it, except as a means of celebrating festivity. Those who enjoy a drink are mostly men belonging to the "intellectual class"; yet they drink only with their meals, if they drink at all. Never would they call for a drink either before meal or after it, except, of course, those who have acquired a Western habit. There is no such thing as a public house. You may order drinks at an inn or a restaurant, but you must order food at the same time. No drink is served by itself. Drunkenness in the proper sense of the term is almost unknown and one finds in vain any record of such an offence in any judicial annal, ancient or modern. Because of this, and because the Chinese in general have not only no craze for drink but also have no capacity for it, a person who has a great capacity, as distinguished from a habit, is rather admired, as if he were specially gifted by Nature like those heroes or great poets one reads about in old romances or is traditionally told. Therefore to say that a person has an "Oceanic Capacity" for wine is a high compliment. If, however, you say that he "drinks like a fish", as I have once heard

---

1. For full poem see *East and West,* by the same author, pp. 54-5

it said by a person highly placed who apparently knew more English than Chinese, it is, of course, offensive.

As wine drinking has seldom been abused in China, no Chinese sage has ever condemned it. According to Confucius, "There is no limit in (the drinking of) wine, but one must not get drunk (*Luann*)."[1] This precept is considered by the Chinese as wise. For if it were "Thou shalt not drink", it would, like trying to enjoin celibacy on a whole people, be "more honour'd in the breach than the observance". Traditionally, the blame for plucking the apple of Eden was put on Eve, but if Adam had been in the garden long enough he would have plucked it too. About 3,500 years ago, when wine was first invented and presented to the Emperor, he tasted it and probably drank more than he should and, feeling the effect of it, decreed Prohibition. China may thus be said to be the country which first tried Prohibition law, but the attempt soon proved futile and only made the "forbidden fruit sweetest". It is therefore wiser and more effective to say to the people, "You may drink but you must not get drunk"; because such counsel or injunction, being human and reasonable, will more likely be followed or obeyed. Thus a Chinese, in declining another glass, would politely say, "I have already drunk to my capacity." Sometimes he would say, "I am already '*Tzuey*' (i.e. have already exceeded my capacity)."

The Chinese word "*Tzuey*" needs an explanation. According to the dictionary it is translated as "drunk" and vice versa. This is apt to be misleading. In general, it means "up to, or exceeding, the limit of one's capacity" without connoting any of that ugliness associated with being "drunk" in the common acceptation of the term. Even in polite society, a person may

---

1. *Confucius: Lun Yu*, Pt. X, Ch. 8.

"soberly" say that he is "*Tzuey*". The proper word for "drunk", therefore, is "*Luann*" ("*Luenn*" in Cantonese), as given in the Confucian precept, already quoted, or "*Shiuh*", as given in the *Book of History*. For that reason, though the word "*Tzuey*" appears very often in Chinese poetry, it must not be thought that Chinese poets are drunkards. A Chinese writing to an intimate friend would often say, "One day we will have a *Tzuey* together," meaning really to have a meal together and drink to hearts' content, as an expression of cordiality and warmth of friendship. Of course, poets like *Li Tai Po*, whose poetry is well known to Western scholars, are exceptions. He would write lively as follows:

> "Be gay when thou art in a happy tone.
> Let not an empty bottle face the moon.
> God gave us the talents not in vain.
> A thousand ducats spent shall come again.
> From ancient times all sages have been dry.
> But drinkers leave their names that never die."[1]

This testifies to the spirit of the poet rather than lays down a precept by him, like the following lines by Dr. Johnson:

> "Say, then, physicians of each kind,
> Who cure the body and the mind.
> What harm in drinking can there be,
> Since punch and life so well agree?"

As is well known, wine, properly speaking, is a form of alcoholic drink made from grapes — an art in which the French excel. Unfortunately, the Chinese vocabulary has only one word, "*Jeou*", for all forms of alcoholic drinks, whether the sort

---

1. First translated in *China Moulded by Confucius*, by the same author, p.103

of drink is wine properly so-called, whiskey, beer, brandy, gin, or liqueur, though in modern days those who have had contact with the West would sometimes qualify the word *Jeou* with a word indicating the particular kind of alcoholic drink he means, such as "Beer *Jeou*" or "Brandy *Jeou*". If you look up a dictionary, however, the word *Jeou* is generally translated as "wine" and vice versa, though a well-compiled dictionary would translate the word "wine" as "*Jeou* made from grapes". But it is wine all the same. Thus it often happens that a Westerner, who is guest at a Chinese party and is asked whether he takes wine, is often, to his surprise, given beer, whiskey, or brandy; presumably he is offered foreign "wine".

Strictly speaking, therefore, China has no wine, at least in origin. It was only at the end of the last century that she began to make wine, properly so-called, in Chefoo, where the grapes are of high quality, but the quantity produced is limited and its quality cannot be compared with that of French wine. What is native to China is made from rice or *Gao Liang*. The best known "rice-wine" is called "yellow wine", because of its golden colour. Sometimes it is called "*Shao Shing*", which is the name of the district where it is made, just as French wine is often known by the name of the place where it is produced. To make "wine" from rice is very common in China. For instance, people in Canton make such wine in different forms, some of which are rather strong, others rather sweet. "Wine" made in various forms from *Gao Liang* is confined to the northern part of the country. It is very strong, equivalent in strength to Vodka or rather stronger. According to modern classification it is really a liqueur and should be drunk as such; but people in the North drink it just like wine, probably because the climate is cold.

The "yellow wine" is mild, equivalent in strength to mild sherry and tastes like it, so much so that if you use it instead of sherry for cooking, no one would notice the difference. To be good, it should be at least seven years old; when it is really mature, which would require about fifteen years, it is exquisite, having the bouquet of that famous French wine *Château-Yquem*, minus the sweetness. It should always be drunk lukewarm, more than *Chambré*, but not hot as some people would make it and thus spoil it. It is the ideal drink to accompany Chinese food. In order to give my Western friends an idea of its nature as a form of drink, I often say that it has all the virtues of sherry and none of its vices. Once I said this to a distinguished English Admiral, and he, apparently a "defender" of sherry, asked me solemnly, "What vice has sherry?" To calm him, I said: "My dear Admiral, don't take this too tragically. Sherry in my opinion, however dry it may be, is *inclined* to be sweet, and however mild it may be, is *inclined* to be heavy. No one, for instance, would think of drinking one bottle of sherry and, still less two, however excellent it may be. But in the case of the "yellow wine", you are expected to drink one at least and two when you are in a good mood. I know an eminent compatriot of yours who one evening drank three at my house in Nanking without even once leaving the table!"

It may seem strange, but it is a fact, that re-

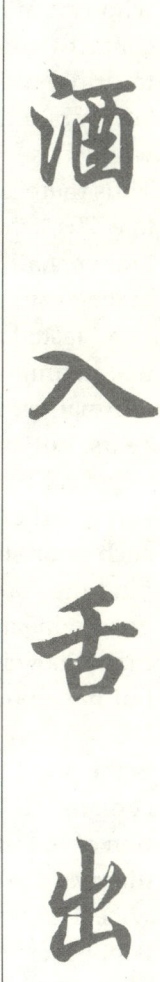

ally good "yellow wine" is almost unobtainable in a place like Shanghai except from private cellars; because, there, those who can afford to pay a high price have generally been in contact with Western civilization and so think it fashionable to drink, or have acquired the habit of drinking, beer, whiskey, or brandy (but rarely wine, except, perhaps, champagne), while those who cannot afford to spend much have no choice. Thus there is no market for good native wine. One day in the late '20s, when I practised law in Shanghai, I went to a well-known native wine-shop in Nanking Road and asked the manager whether he had really good "yellow wine", such as I had tasted in Peking, adding that he could charge any price that he might think reasonable. He replied with an emphatic affirmative, and said that his shop had a history of over fifty years. But after trying samples from almost a dozen jars I rejected all with unequivocal reasons, as well as unconcealed surprise that a shop of such standing as his should have only such poor stuff. "Sir," said he, rising stately from his seat behind the counter, "the wines that you have just tasted are all good wine according to the standard that obtains in this cosmopolitan city. I have been in this shop for nearly thirty years but have never met a customer who is so particular as you. We certainly have what you would call good wine, but what is the good of stocking it here? A jar of wine, as you know, contains about ten gallons. A person like you may buy a fraction of it, but the rest will be wasted or has to be sold like ordinary wine of the day; for there is no demand for high-priced wine. People nowadays, because they can speak a tongue that is not their own, drink only what is imported from abroad. They don't know the good things of their own country." He spoke the last sentence with such undisguised disgust that I could not help dropping a sympathetic sigh. Then, very friendly, he said that his shop had a few jars lying at the bottom of the cellar from time "immemorial", and that he would let me have them at a reasonable price, but that I must wait for the stock to clear, which would take a few months. I gladly accepted the offer and he faithfully fulfilled his promise. The wine was delicious. It also had an interesting sequel. First, he made a special effort afterwards in procuring some mature wine to stock in his shop for me and customers introduced by me. He never knew who I was except as a lawyer; so he labelled this special wine as "Lawyer's Wine", which gradually became well known and the shop did a good trade. Secondly, one day late in the afternoon, an eminent member of the Bar, a friend of mine, hurriedly called at my office with an anxious face. I thought he had come to consult me on a point of foreign law, with which he was not familiar, or to ask me to co-operate in a big case. To my pleasant surprise, which would touch one's poetic vein, he said: "I don't know what to do this evening. I have guests but no good wine. Can you lend me some of that delicious wine I drank at your dinner the other night?"

"Well, my friend," said I, "I thought law was a prosaic profession. Now, I am meeting *Li Tai-Po* in my chambers. I had four jars from the shop and have already consumed one with friends. Your request is too poetic for words. Wine is not to be borrowed but to be shared with those who enjoy it. You are welcome

to have one full jar!" I never saw a happier smile than what flashed over his face at my remark. This recalls a similar incident that occurred when I was Vice-Minister of Justice in Nanking. One day, I received from the Prime Minister of the day a very poetic letter accompanied by a box of cigars. It asked for a loan, or rather for an exchange with the cigars, of some of my wine that he had tasted! He was the same personage who called on me with a poem specially written by him on my fiftieth birthday, as quoted in my *East and West*.[1]

I have said that from private cellars one can get very good wine even in Shanghai. There is a custom pretty general in China that, when a child is born, jars of wine, which vary in number with the means of the family, are stored away not to be opened until the child gets married. Such wine is not a merchandise; but, when it is due to be drunk, its maturity and bouquet can well be imagined. . . .

As Peking (of course, the Peking I knew) has been for centuries the Capital of China and therefore the centre of culture, it is also the market for good wine. But Chinese wine merchants, like dealers in *objets d'art*, are apt to have their own way of treating their customers. A dealer in art, at least in China, would sell a rare piece, for a lesser price, to a connoisseur rather than, for a higher price, to one who knows nothing about art but only collects merely for the sake of collecting; because he feels that, in the possession of the former, the object will be prized and well taken care of, so that though its ownership has changed, he can still retain the notion that he has not parted with it for ever; whereas, in the possession of the latter, he would feel that it is entirely lost to him. He regards an art treasure as if it were his own female child; he would,

---

1. Pp. 151-52

other considerations being equal, marry her rather to one who has only moderate means but loves her than to one who is blessed with a larger fortune but is only keen in possessing her.

The wine merchant has ideas similar to those of the art dealer but more "poetic". If by chance he has come by some unique wine—that is, extremely old wine acquired from private cellars—he would, in retail, sell it, unmixed with younger wine, only to connoisseurs known to him. A person not known to him as such, though he pays the same price or even more, unless he buys the whole jar unopened, will often not get exactly the same wine. For instance, he may mix 15-year-old wine with 40-year-old wine and call it 40 years old. This is in fact often done in wine sold in retail; for Chinese wines of the same class do mix well and, according to the price charged and the age reputed, this can only be the case; otherwise the wine would be sold at a loss, just as no sensible person who buys a bottle of so-called Napoleon brandy would think that it had been bottled in the time of the battle of Trafalgar or Waterloo. What may be of interest is the wine merchant's moral justification of his "discrimination". His philosophical reasoning is somewhat like this: "If a person is not a connoisseur, he can never tell the difference between the various degrees of nicety due to age. So long as the wine is really good and far better than any that he has

ever tasted, it is the same to him whether it is 20, 30 or 40 years old. Really old wine is very rare and difficult to obtain, and to sell it in retail is often at a loss. In order to do justice to the wine and to prevent waste of good and rare things, it is only right that unique wine should be reserved for those who do and can appreciate it."

Thus it happened that one day in the '20s a prominent Cabinet Minister of the day, a friend of mine, had to ask me by telephone to oblige him by ordering from a certain wine shop some wine, then known as "1875", which he had drunk at my house but which his butler could never get from the same shop.

A word of explanation of the possibility of such "discrimination" is, perhaps, necessary. Chinese wine is preserved in an earthenware jar which generally holds about ten gallons. Its "vintage", that is the year in which it was made, is testified in a slip of paper hidden under the earth cover of the jar. To open the jar, you first remove the earth cover and you will find the slip. Therefore, unless you buy the whole jar (a thing one rarely does, because, once the jar is opened, the wine will keep only for a few months) you have only the words of the wine merchant to depend on for the "vintage". For this reason a connoisseur who buys wine in retail would first taste the wine at the shop and base his judgment on the taste test rather than on the "vintage" professed.

Wine which tastes *as if* it were bitter is the best. When it tastes *as if* it were salty, it is also good. If it tastes sour, it is bad. When it tastes sweet, it is worse.

I happened to know a retired scholar-statesman of the *Ch-*

ing dynasty who was a Cantonese and therefore my co-provincial. Through him I came to know Prince Lun — the man who was twice barred from succeeding to the Throne owing to the intrigue of the Empress Dowager — and a Mongolian Prince, Official Head of the Mongolians and Tibetans under the Chinese Government. We four formed a "Fortnightly Dining Group", doing host in turn. It was in this way and through this scholar-statesman that I became a "privileged" client of a certain wine shop, which almost exclusively had occasionally some rare wine acquired from private cellars. As this could only be of a limited quantity, it was always reserved for the "privileged few".

On the ethical plane, discarding the commercial consideration of loss and profit, this "discrimination" of the wine merchant may be questionable. But his motive of preventing waste and of reserving the best for the most appreciative is not undeserving of commendation.

I was told a personal story by a man who held a high position in an international institution and belongs to a race noted for wit and humour. Not long after the First World War he was sent to Eastern Europe on a mission which entailed a great deal of entertainment. At his first official banquet he gave orders that the best liqueur brandy should be served, but

to his surprise very few guests took it. At his next banquet he told the *maître d'hôtel* that "Hennessy Three Stars" should be served and he found that everybody enjoyed it. In telling this story with all the humour characteristic of his race, he said, "I saved a lot of money too!" I also know a man who keeps three kinds of cigars: one for those who are connoisseurs, one for those who are not connoisseurs but really enjoy good cigars, and one he himself daily smokes, and this is also what he would give to those who smoke cigars but cannot say they enjoy them. He asked me one day whether his "discrimination" was justified. I said: "This is only good sense. Indeed, you are already very generous by offering what you yourself smoke to men of the last category, thus conforming to the precept 'Love thy neighbour as thyself!' "

CHAPTER ELEVEN

Dining as an Art

IT is only commonplace to say that dining as a pleasure to life does not consist entirely in the food itself, though it may be the principal factor; for the simple reason that, without food, or rather good food, there would be no dining and the pleasure would be of a different kind. All the elaborate arrangements and decorations made in preparation for a State banquet, for instance, though they have much to do with the importance and dignity of the occasion, are not devoid of the motive, conscious or unconscious, of making dining an art; otherwise it might be sufficient merely to stage the dinner in a historical hall and serve it on gold plates without all the artistic decorations that tend to heighten the sense of gaiety and festivity. Indeed, music is often employed and beauty invoked, so that all the senses may be appealed to and enlivened. This art was, perhaps, more emphasized in ancient days when rulers could do almost what they liked. Thus we have the story of the historic origin of the English Order of the Garter and the film showing Henry VIII, wrestling with a wrestler in the presence of his Queen and others, as "cum-dinner" entertainment. In various degrees and in different manners, the art of entertainment must have been cultivated by all nations in all ages. China being an ancient country with the dawn of her civilization at an early date, ceremony — a mark of culture — also plays a part. In pre-Republican days, such ceremony was very elaborate, but interesting enough to be recounted:

1. The host stands on the west side of the hall a few yards from the dinner table.
2. The "Master of Ceremony" bows to the guest of honour and conducts him to a place on the east side of the hall not far from but opposite to where the host is standing.
3. The host bows to the guest, who bows in return.
4. The host ascends the hall up to the dinner table and bows to the empty chair on which the guest is to sit. The guest, now facing the host, bows in return.
5. The host walks to the chair and, with both sleeves, touches the cushion of the chair as a symbol of dusting it. After this, he bows to the chair and the guest bows in return.
6. The host, with a bow, raises the pair of chopsticks to be used by the guest, who bows in return.
7. The host, with a bow, raises the wine cup to be used by the guest, who bows in return.
8. The host returns to the place where he stood and bows to the guest, who bows in return.
9. The guest leaves and is conducted to his seat.

During this ceremony a solemn but cheerful music is played, while the eyes of all, in dead silence, are concentrated on the performance and try to catch a glimpse of the guest of honour. Though consisting of a few bows, the sight is full of meaning, dignified, and beautiful. If negotiation of a treaty, for instance, were to take place after a meal clothed with such formality, it is inconceivable that the negotiators would use such unceremonial language as sometimes employed by certain diplomats in international conferences in recent time. They may, indeed, disagree, but they would agree to disagree.

However, it is not the formal kind of entertainment that forms the theme here; for this,
though interesting, does not make part of the
living or life of the people. It is the informal
entertainment, the daily affair, that the Chinese have, through the ages, cultivated to a
fine art. In philosophic reasoning, the Chinese
often use the phrase, "Heaven, Earth, and
People", meaning that success of every kind
depends, in various degrees, on three factors,
namely *Opportunity* or *Time* (which is afforded
by Heaven), *Right Place* (Earth), and *Support or
Co-operation of Others* (People), of which the
lack of one may bring you within sight of success but will prevent you from reaching the
goal. Though this is never formally invoked
in the art of dining, it is in fact often applied.
Hence in giving a dinner one chooses the occasion or time, the place and the guests, in order to make it a success. The occasion or time
factor is most flexible. Realizing that there can
be no control over the element, the Chinese,
with his philosophy, adapts himself to it by
some reasoning (which may appear poetical
to some or plausible to others), turning what
may otherwise be a miserable day into an occasion for enjoyment.

Thus one may receive an impromptu invitation for celebrating the snow or the rain (provided of course that neither is a disastrous
one!) If the invitation has something to do
with the weather, the dishes should, accord-

ing to Chinese ideas, in some way accord with the nature of the purpose. For instance, on a rainy day there should be, as a contrast, more dry (such as deep-fry, roast, or grilled) dishes than soupy ones. In a snowy night nothing would be more appropriate than the Chinese chafing dish, which consists of various kinds of meat, sea food, and vegetable, of which all are raw and cut in suitable sizes ready to be cooked to one's own liking at the table in a vessel with seasoned soup over a stove with red-hot charcoal. The sight of the smokeless fire, the heat emitting from it, and the steam engendered by the bubbling soup contrast vividly with the snow-flakes falling down or flying about outside the window. It is good fun, too, that every one round the table has something to do. There is no question of "too many cooks spoiling the broth". The soup resulting from this "communal" cooking is in fact delicious.

The next factor is the place where the dinner is to be staged. In winter the home with the fireside naturally occurs to oneself. In other seasons, if the weather permits, the garden lit up with lanterns or a pavilion surrounded by trees or, when certain popular flowers are in season, such as peony, chrysanthemum, plum blossoms, jasmine, lilac, etc., a place within sight of these would often form the Chinese choice. There are in China lakes and rivers equipped with pleasure-boats, such as the West Lake in Hang Chow, the Chin Huai River in Nanking, the Pearl River in Canton, etc.: a dinner staged on such a boat on a moonlit or starry night, with intermittent music coming from the neighbouring boats or a distant hut, while one's own boat is cruising around, is enchanting and makes a special appeal to those who appreciate the art of dining. This art must have been developed at an early age in China, as witnessed in the following *Tang* poem:

"There came abruptly through the streaming foam
The *Pi-Par* sound of dainty ancient art

....

....

Tracing the sound we wondered who it was.
The music stopped, as someone wished to speak.
Forthwith we steered our boat in changed course.
A meeting with the Muse we fain would seek.

We dressed our table with fresh food and wines.
All lights gone out were lit up once again.

....

...."

The third factor is the guests. As indiscriminate invitation, merely for the sake of invitation, may sometimes lead to unforeseen incidents embarrassing both to the host and to the guests, one invites on a purely social and informal occasion those and only those who, one thinks, can happily meet. To ensure that nothing may have been overlooked, it has long been a practice in China to accompany the invitation with a list of the names of the persons invited, so that every guest may know beforehand whom he is going to meet, and if by chance there is among the other guests someone whom he does not wish to meet, he can decline.

When these "three factors" are decided upon, the next question is the food and wine, to which a Chinese host is, in general, rather attentive, and this must be the case with all hosts; for if the food is not good there can be no entertainment and, however sumptuous the meal may be, there can be no great pleasure at the table if the wine is indifferent. In the matter of wine the palm must be given to the French both for its qualities and for its varieties. But for Chinese food, the good "yellow wine", as mentioned in the previous chapter, is without a rival. Here again the law of Nature is at work. A nation which has developed a cuisine like the Chinese must, as a logical sequel, have also discovered or invented some form of drink that particularly suits its own food. However, as a substitute, a good claret or Burgundy may do. So may a very dry white wine, but not champagne.

In the choice of food the Chinese cuisine is a fruitful source. There are dishes for every season, not so simple as hot things on cold days and cold things on hot days, but composed of things in season and prepared in such a way that they bring the season to one's senses or though hot, they impart coolness to the eye. But just because there is a great variety of things to choose, the choice is sometimes difficult. It is no exaggeration that the drafting of a good menu, like drafting an agenda for an international conference, requires thought and experience. The occasion, the season, and the taste of the guests need to be considered. It would not do, for instance, to offer the same things to the English or, in general, the Americans as may be offered to the French. Even among the Chinese themselves, as there are several Schools of cooking in China, the taste of the people of one province varies from that of another. However, in a full-course Chinese dinner, which generally consists of ten to twelve courses, every main form of cooking should, as far as possible, he represented, such as steaming, deep-frying, *Chow* (low-oil-quick-stir-frying), roasting, stewing, grilling, *Duonn* (double-saucepan cooking), etc., and the materials used should also be representative, such as sea food, meat, poultry and/or game, and vegetables, apart from two or three special delicacies. One may ask why there should be so many courses. The answer is fourfold:

1. The conventional number of guests including the host is from ten to twelve, who all cannot be expected to like the same thing. Therefore the greater the number of dishes, the greater the choice for the guests.

2. Variety is the essence of a Chinese meal. The change from one taste to another at short intervals enhances the appetite and avoids the feeling of excess due to eating only one or two things in a comparatively large quantity; for in a Chinese dinner one takes only a suitable quantity of each as one would do in eating *hors d'œuvres*.

3. A guest is not obliged by any rule of good manners to eat every dish or much of it, but it is quite in order to have a second, third, or fourth helping, if he happens to like any particular dish.

4. To eat hurriedly is not to enjoy a good meal. A great number of dishes in suitable proportion, served at proper intervals, prolongs the enjoyment and gives more opportunities for conversation.

The order in which the dishes should be served is also a matter of art. To have them served indiscriminately would be like delivering a well-conceived or well-prepared speech in an indifferent manner or rather like marshalling badly the facts of a case in pleading

to a jury. It would not do, for instance, to have two soupy or "heavy" dishes, or one roast and one grilled dishes, served one after the other. The charm of variety and contrast applies to the order in which the dishes are served no less than to the dishes themselves. Nay, even the proportion of some dishes merits attention. What is reputed to be expensive, if served in a comparatively large quantity, looks grand and heightens the appetite; what is known to be cheap, however exquisitely prepared, looks valuable only when it is served in a relatively small portion.

Entertainment of the guests, apart from food and wine, at the dinner, as distinguished from after it, is a matter which, it is conceivable, varies in different countries in conformity with their conventions. But as one must talk, conversation is naturally a means common to all. In the West the art of conversation is highly prized, though how far it is still culti- vated — England for instance — since the days of Dr. Johnson and his contemporaries may be questioned. The Chinese are just as keen as others in displaying wit at the table, but they would not go so far as to have their conversations prepared, for affectation and artificiality are generally despised. Thanks to the round-table, they have the advantage of being able to speak to all at more or less the same distance, whereas in the West, where in general a long table is used, one can speak conveniently only to one's immediate neighbour. However, in China, games are often played as a means of inducing the guests to drink; for the Chinese rarely drink alone or without being "urged". The most popular game is the "fin- ger game", called by the Cantonese "Guess the Unknown", which is open to and played by all. It is played, I have been told, also in Italy and called *Mora*, probably introduced into that country by Marco Polo. However, the Chinese rules of the game differ from the Italian in the fact that, according to the former, it is the loser who has to drink, whereas, according to the latter, it is the winner. The Chinese concept of the game, therefore, is more sporting; for according to it, since the winner has already had the honour of winning, the loser should be given the consolation of having a drink. This "consolation" is often mistaken in these days for a penalty, but this is not the original meaning, inasmuch as the winner sometimes drinks with the loser at the same time.

The game deserves some notice. It is a test of intelligence, at least in a particular field, and, like chess, was probably invented as a game in military science; for it involves quick guessing, immediate decision, tactics, ruse, and strategy, applied all at the same time. It is played between two persons, each of whom throws out at the same time one hand, either closed or open with one, two, three, four, or five fingers, and calls a number, which, in order to win, should be the exact, total number of fingers issued by you and your opponent. For instance, you throw out your hand open with three fingers and call "six". This means that you guess that your opponent will also issue three fingers; otherwise, the total number would not make "six". If, however, he issues four fingers and calls "seven", or five fingers and call "eight", or none and calls "three", he will win; because the total number of fingers

issued by him and you in each of these instances corresponds to the number he has called. If neither of you guesses the number right, there is "no game", and it will continue until one of you has guessed it right. And if both of you guess it right, this is called "draw", and the game continues just as if it were "no game". It should be mentioned that, as there can be only ten fingers in all, the highest number you can call is "ten"; and you will win by calling "ten" if both you and your opponent throw out an open hand with five fingers; because they make "ten". And as one may throw out a closed hand, issuing no finger, you may win by calling "none" if both you and your opponent happen to throw out only a closed hand issuing no finger.

In the light of the above explanation of the game it is clear that the first thing you have to do, in playing the game, is to guess, before showing your own hand, how many fingers your opponent is most likely to issue, so that you may issue the proper number of your own fingers or none at all in order to make up the number you call and win. Your opponent will naturally do the same. Thus, in order to dodge your opponent or mislead him, you employ tactics, ruse or strategy, or all these at the same time. Very often, after a few games, you have spotted a recurrent, technically known as "dead", number on the part of your opponent — that is, the number of fingers he is fond of issuing or the number he is fond of calling. In that cast you will try to "catch" that number or dodge it, as the case may be, to your own advantage. In this game I have in my younger days met a man who could play blindfolded with you and win 19 games out of 20, if not all. In my *East and West* I have compared him to Prince Florizel of Bohemia in *The Rajah's Diamond* of Robert Louis Stevenson's *New Arabian Nights*. He was a scholar, poet, brilliant conversationalist, and, indeed, marvellous man.

Another game is known as "Wine Command". It is rather literary in nature. For example, a word is chosen, and each person has by turn clockwise to recite from a chosen book— say, the *Tang* poems or the *Confucian Analects*—a sentence in which that particular word occurs, and the place in which it occurs determines who will have to drink, as counted from the reciter. He who fails to do so is "fined" one drink and the next person takes the turn. As an illustration let the word be "Friend", the book be *Julius Caesar*, and the number of persons at the table be ten, A to J.

A: "But let not therefore my good *friends* be grieved."[1]
G drinks, being seventh from A.

B: "So we are Caesar's *friends* that have abridged."[2]
F drinks, being fifth from B.

C: "Will you be pick'd in number of our *friends*."[3]
A drinks, being ninth from C.

D: "And in the pulpit, as becomes a *friend*."[4]
A drinks again, being eighth from D.

E: "Then follow me, and give me audience, *friends*."[5]
B drinks, being eighth from E.

Limitation to one book is sometimes felt rather too restrict-

---

1. Act I, Sc. 2, l. 41.
2. Act III, Sc.1, l. 103.
3. *Ibid.*, l. 216.
4. Act III, Sc. 1, l. 229.
5. Act III, Sc. 2, l, 2.

ed, so other books may be included. Let Longfellow, Milton, *Hamlet*, Tennyson, and Pope be added.

F: "No chance of birth or place has made us *friends*."[6]
E drinks, being tenth from F.

G: "He leaves his gods, his *friends*, and native soil."[7]
B drinks, being sixth from G.

H: "For who not needs shall never lack a *friend*."[8]
F drinks, being ninth from H.

I: "And *friend* slew *friend* not knowing whom he slew."[9]
J and B drink, being second and fourth from I respectively.

J: "Statesman, yet *friend* to truth! of soul sincere."[10]
B drinks, being third from J.

Such a game is, of course, very interesting to scholars but would be unfair and even embarrassing to those who are not. Therefore more often games open to all are played (apart from the "finger game"), such as counting numbers in an intriguing way or answering questions asked by the "Toast Master" from a card drawn by a guest. The answer is in the form of "Yes" or "No". An amusing instance is the question, "Are you henpecked?" If you answer "Yes" you will be "fined" one drink; but if you answer "No", you will be "fined" two! A game like this can, of course, be played only for one round, since repetition, like a tale once told, would beget no interest. However,

---

6. Longfellow, *The Seaside and the Fireside.*
7. Milton, *Paradise Lost.*
8. *Hamlet,* Act III, Sc. 1, l. 199.
9. Tennyson, *The Passing of Arthur.*
10. Pope, *Moral Essays.*

as China is the country where scholarship is most prized, it is the scholars by whom the art of dining is most cultivated. Apart from the not unusual experience that dining is used as a means of fostering the literary art, history is full of instances of the finest poems being written at the dinner table as a result of the ecstasy engendered by the art of entertainment. The best known case happened in the *Tang* dynasty, and the story is:

A scholar official had rebuilt a famous, historic building in the province of Kiangsi. To celebrate the completion of the work, he invited many high officials and known scholars of the day to a dinner staged in the artistic surroundings of the new building with the intention of displaying at a suitable moment the scholarship of his son-in-law, who was a scholar of repute. As planned, the latter prepared and committed to memory a long poem of a special style in honour of the new building. The "plot" was that, towards the end of the dinner, when every guest had had his share of the bottle, he would send for paper, pen, and ink, and ask the guests by turn to do him the honour of writing a long poem on the spot as a souvenir of the occasion, hoping that all of them would decline, so that when he came to the last guest, his son-in-law, the latter would accept the "challenge" and write out the poem he had already prepared. To his surprise and annoyance, when these writing

materials reached a young man of nineteen, the most junior of all, who was there only by accident, being on his way to visit his father, he took up the "challenge" without further ado. The host, highly displeased inwardly, seeing his "literary plot" being frustrated, sent someone to peep over the young man's shoulder to see what he was writing. On being informed of the first few verses written, he murmured, "Nothing extraordinary." But on receipt of further report he exclaimed: "This is genius! My son-in-law could never be equal to it." He was particularly impressed by two lines, which may be rendered as follows:

"Descending mist along with lonely petrel flew,
The autumn water matching boundless sky in blue."

This long poem has become a classic and is read by all.

Dining as an art is cultivated not only in the home but also objectively in the restaurant, especially in Peking of old. In this respect, as far as I know, some of the small but well-known restaurants in Paris come very near to those restaurants in Peking in which that art is most developed. It has nothing to do with the display of silver or surrounding you with a group of waiters like bodyguards. It is the creation of a communal atmosphere among the customers, so that everyone feels at home and inclined to be cheerful. Indeed, the atmosphere is such that one sometimes feels as if one were participating in a wedding feast or Christmas dinner with the other customers. It is an invisible art that must have taken centuries to develop, so much so that it is easier to appreciate than to explain or describe, because it is embodied in the heart of those who serve you and reveals itself naturally. Two instances suffice:

One day in Paris an old friend, a diplomat, invited me to dinner at one of the small restaurants well known for good food. Being a connoisseur, he had ordered beforehand two bottles of wine of good vintage and reserved a table. On arrival we saw the wine being properly *chambré* on the mantelpiece. Wishing to taste the wine but unable to find the wine waiter, one of his secretaries, a connoisseur in wine, went to open one of the bottles himself. Just as he was doing this, the wine waiter passed by. He did not interfere or go away, but stopped and watched attentively until the cork was carefully drawn. Then he smilingly left, showing a visible relief. He did not interfere, because he saw the man trying to open the bottle was holding it in the right way. He did not go away, because he held himself ready for any "emergency". He felt a relief, because he saw the cork properly drawn without shaking the bottle and thus disturbing the wine. All this showed how much importance he attached to a bottle of good wine and how heartily he shared the pleasure of his customers.

One evening years ago I was dining in the "Mongolian" restaurant in Peking, quite familiar to Europeans and Americans who have lived in the capital, and well known for crabs and for mutton cooked in a chafing dish or grilled over an open fire. The restaurant was then almost full, as it was always. Then came an old man of strong physique, recalling the image of Samson of the Bible. As soon as he had sat down he ordered, apart from other things, ten plates of mutton, equivalent to about one and a half pounds of meat, and ten jugs of *Gao Liang*, equivalent in quantity and in strength to a full bottle of gin. The waiter asked him, "Sir, how many guests have you?" To this he replied, "I am alone!" Thereupon the waiter bowed to him deeply with great reverence, feeling no doubt that he was at last in the presence of one of those great heroes he had read of in novels. The old man soon, but in no haste, finished all that had been brought to him and gave fresh orders, which were swiftly executed, while the waiter was in full attention, standing by. When he ordered the twentieth plate of mutton, the waiter was in such an ecstasy that he sang the order down to the man on the ground floor, whose duty was to receive orders, in a most musical tone, as if to accompany the order with musical honour. As far as I can remember, his words were (in Chinese, of course):

"The grand old man has finished his last plate.
Send what he ordered not a minute late."

To give an idea of his musical tone, it may be transcribed as follows:

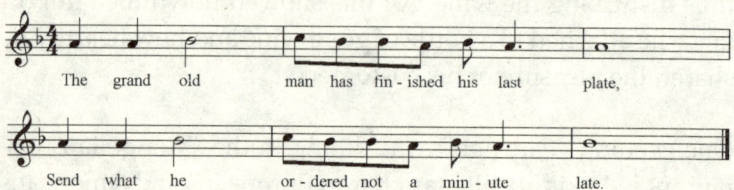

This enthusiasm of the waiter must not be taken as impudence. In Peking of old singing was very popular; because for centuries the Imperial Court had been a great patron of theatrical art. Therefore to be able to sing well was a mark of culture and often a means to "get on". From the Empress Dowager downward in the Manchu Court, it is believed, everybody was able to sing. Prince Lun, who has been mentioned, was a perfect singer and often sang when we dined together. So was his younger brother, who sometimes even took part in a private or charity performance. It was not an unusual phenomenon in those days that the host or the guests would sing between dishes at the dinner table even in a restaurant, or that, when a person was in a playful mood, he answered your questions in a theatrical tone. To use a metaphor, suppose a restaurant waiter in the Vatican should repeat a customer's order in Latin, no one could say that he was impudent, inasmuch as Latin is daily spoken in the Holy City, though, perhaps, in a different circle. To sum up, the art of dining involves the application of the philosophy of "Heaven, Earth, and People", as explained at the commencement of this chapter, and, at its zenith, can make every occasion as enjoyable as Christmas or New Year's Eve.

CHAPTER TWELVE
A Discourse on Tea

I WAS once asked by an eminent English scholar what I thought to be the grimmest sentence. I said: "May it not be the words of Sir Edward (afterwards Lord) Grey, spoken on the eve of the First World War: 'The lamps are going out all over Europe. We shall not see them lit again in our lifetime'?" Immediately, I added: "I should, perhaps, have quoted the Chinese saying, 'There is no feast that does not come to an end.' " Yes, Grey's words, grim as they are, depict only a particular situation, catastrophic, no doubt; but the Chinese saying embodies a grimness that applies to all and is ever true. However powerful an individual or glorious an empire may be, the end *will* come. So does a feast, though it may be very well planned and sumptuous, with all the delicacies described and explained in previous chapters. In the West, the pleasure is prolonged by coffee and the fine products of France in various names and in bottles of various shapes; in China, however, tea and tea alone is drunk at the end of a meal, because Chinese tea, with its fragrant aroma and varieties, is the most fitting beverage after Chinese food. Thanks to this, the Chinese, as explained in a previous chapter, are the soberest nation of the world.

Tea was discovered by the Chinese in the *Tang* dynasty (A.D. 618-906), and its discovery is a great contribution to the pleasures of mankind. It is invigorating, digestive, pleasant to drink, more natural as a beverage than any that is concocted by human device, and, according to Prof. Erich von Knaff-Lenz, is "good for intellectuals".[1] During the Second World War, when China was still fighting a lonely battle against aggression, an English schoolboy asked his father at breakfast what China had done for the world which deserved their support and sympathy. The latter, pointing to the plates on the table and the teacup he was holding, replied: "Has not China taught us to make all these beautiful things now named after her, and has she not given us this delicious beverage which we drink every morning and in the afternoon?" Tea is drunk by the Chinese not only after every meal and not necessarily at any particular time like "afternoon tea", but at all times if a drink is desired. It is a national drink to the highest as well as the humblest. When one visits a person in China he is as a rule offered a cup of tea as a sign of welcome. Whether it is drunk or not is another matter.

Some years after the Washington Conference it was my privilege and official duty to accompany the delegates of different Powers in an International Commission to visit Chinese courts and prisons in various provinces. One day, which happened to be unusually hot, we arrived at the High Court of a certain province. We were received by the Chief Justice into the *salon*. Soon after we had been seated, cups of tea were served. Thereupon, one of the delegates, no doubt very devoted to duty and, perhaps, also affected by the climate, became rather excited, exclaiming, "We are not going to have tea; we have work to do!"

"Monsieur," said I to him, "with this (the tea) you are welcome as a guest; without it you would be treated like a trespasser!"

---

1. See an article by A. M. Rosenthal in the *New York Times,* January 1953.

In Anglo-Saxon jurisprudence the law of negligence says one must not "lay a trap" for those who are on one's premises by invitation, meaning that one will be liable to such persons but not to trespassers for injuries incurred due to defects that should have been seen to. If the Chinese custom were adopted, it would be an interesting point of law whether a would-be trespasser would cease to be such and should be regarded as a person by invitation after he had been served with a cup of tea. However, the custom that tea is a sign of welcome is so universal in China that it once saved a scholar friend of mine from being robbed. He was on a trip by boat to some mining district in the interior. One evening a bandit appeared and, with threats of violence, "arrested" the boat, demanding a search of his belongings. My friend, though a little scared, had the presence of mind to offer the intruder a cup of tea. At the sight of this the latter at once changed his threatening countenance, and, after questioning my friend whether he had any firearms or money, and receiving an answer in the negative—went away, leaving his straw hat behind. My friend relating this incident laughingly said, "Thanks to the cup of tea, I not only lost nothing but also gained something—the hat!"

Although tea drinking is universal among the Chinese, there is no such custom as "tea ceremony" as one sees in Japan. In pre-Republican days, however, there was the practice that, on formal calls in official circles, the raising of the teacup was a gesture that the visit was at an end. In the West, words like "I must not monopolize all your time" are a graceful intimation from Royalties that you may leave, while in less formal circles looking at the watch is often the practice. Different countries naturally have different conventions, but there is much to be said for the old Chinese way, particularly as in those days an official on making a formal call was accompanied by a retinue, who on seeing the teacup raised was able to get ready in time for departure. In any case such a convention cannot be said to be "barbarous". Tea is also used as part of the presents sent to the family of the girl in engagements. It is used because the tea plant would not grow if moved from one place to another. Seeds have to be employed, if one wants to grow tea. This peculiar nature of the tea plant suggests loyalty, oneness, and abidingness — the best symbols of a lasting engagement, preliminary to matrimony. Hence to say that a girl has accepted tea from another means that she is engaged, and to say that she has spilt tea means that she has lost her *fiancé*. Hence also a girl drinking tea would in the old days take good care not to have it upset, a bad omen on a special occasion.

Tea grows almost in all parts of China and there are scores of kinds of tea. Broadly speaking, they fall into two categories: the red or black tea and the green tea, the one being dried over the fire, the other in the sun. The best red teas are *Keemun* (known for its smoothness and delicate aroma) and *Ningchow* (known for its aroma rather than smoothness). Then comes an intermediate class of tea called *Oolung* and *Jasmine*.

All these are well known outside China, while

the best green tea is called the "Dragon's Well" (*Lung Jiing*). But tea, like other commodities, though under the same name, has different qualities. Generally speaking, the earliest crop is the best, because it is the youngest. In the case of the green tea, it is often labelled with the words "Before the rain", that is, the leaves are plucked before rain falls; for the rain has the effect of making the leaves grow fast, and if they were plucked after rain had fallen, they would be coarse and have less flavour. However, there is a special kind of tea little known abroad. It grows on the cliffs of only a few mountains in Amoy. Hence it is generally called "Cliff tea", but labelled, according to its quality, with various Buddhistic names, such as "Iron Goddess of Mercy", "Iron Lo Han", and "Iron Buddha". Because some of it grows on steep cliffs, it used to be said that monkeys were trained to pluck it. Even now some of this tea is labelled with the words "Monkey Pluck". Its production is so limited that it is just enough for home consumption and is the most expensive. It has an exquisite, natural fragrance like perfume, unequalled by that of any other tea, and is drunk in small cups as one would drink liqueur. If you visit a person in Amoy you may be offered this special tea, but if you drink it like drinking beer, the chance is that you will not be offered the same tea next time, unless you have in the meantime cultivated yourself to appreciate it!

Although tea grows in China and the Chinese drink tea at all times of the day, it does not follow that every Chinese knows how to make tea properly, just as diamonds, though produced in Africa and sold largely in London, Paris and New York, are best cut in Amsterdam or Antwerp. By this is not meant that people other than the Chinese can make tea better — far from it. An eminent American tea examiner, who had forty years' experience in his profession, has recently been quoted as saying, "Most American men have never tasted real tea."[1]

"The American woman, for all her education, cook books, and heating appliances, is inadequate to the task of bringing water to a boil. She can compete successfully in business, politics, sports, and the arts, but when it comes to boiling water—the kid hasn't got it."[2] So far as boiling water is concerned, one may be sure that the Chinese woman or man is equal to the task; because it is a general belief among the Chinese, almost amounting to superstition, that to drink water that has not been brought to the boiling point would cause illness. It is the other techniques that not all can be expected to know. Tea, properly speaking, is not merely a mixture of tea leaves and water. For instance, if you have the tea leaves stewed in water, as some people do, the liquid resulting from such a process is not tea in the proper sense: it would be like some sort of medicine. The Russian peasant, I have been told, carries a cake of tea with him and, when he desires a drink, bites a piece of it, chews it, and then drinks some water to wash it down. Such a process does not make tea either.

Tea, properly so called, has to be properly made. Like wine or spirit, it has also a maximum and a minimum in strength, beyond or

---

1. *New York Times,* 17 February, 1953.
2. *New York World-Telegram and Sun,* 16 February, 1953.

below which the mixture will cease to be tea in the proper sense of the word. Therefore the first condition in making tea is to make it in the right strength. He who prefers very weak tea — that is, tea below the normal strength — should dilute it with water after it has been made in the right strength. Even if he makes tea only for himself, this rule should be followed. It would not do to make the tea *ab initio* so abnormally weak to suit his own taste that he may avoid the trouble of diluting it with water. The reason is simple. Some persons drink whisky neat; others drink it with plenty of water. It would not do to have whisky specially made for the latter in such a weak condition that they would be saved the trouble of adding water; for such a liquid, if made, would not be whisky at all. The same applies to tea. Consequently, the proper way of serving tea is to have pot of tea properly made and a pot of very hot water for dilution, if necessary. If one errs, it is better to err on the right side; because, with the hot water ready, there is always the remedy. The way of dilution is to dilute the tea in the cup and not the tea in the pot. To do the latter would be a "wholesale" dilution, leaving no room for adjustment. If, however, there is no more tea but only tea leaves in the teapot, that is a different question and water may be added to it; but this is not diluting the tea; it is having a second helping of it. In order to get the benefit of a second helping, care should also be taken, as in making tea at the beginning, with regard to the amount of water to be added. For the tea thus made is still to be tea, just as in a second marriage the man or woman, though he or she has once been married, is still to be husband or wife as the case may be.

How much tea should be used? Since there are a maximum and a minimum in strength, this leaves room for individual taste. The answer also depends on the kind of tea used — China tea or non-China tea. As in cooking, judgment should be used. In the West, the popular measurement is one teaspoon of tea for each cup and one for the pot. This is perhaps to err on the right side; for if a person makes tea for himself and desires two cups, he will, according to this rule, have to use three teaspoons of tea— which according to experience is excessive. So far as China tea is concerned, one *teaspoonful* for the first cup and a level *teaspoon* for every successive cup (without any for the pot) will be sufficient. For Chinese people, the word person may be substituted for the word cup; for, as they drink tea at all times, they do not, as a rule, drink a large quantity at any time or drink it very strong— the "Golden Mean". It is also worth noting that though the above rule may be strictly followed— one level teaspoon for each cup— the tea made for, say, five persons tastes stronger than that made for, say, two persons, in spite of the fact that the same quantity of tea is allowed for each cup. The reason is, if tea is made for a larger number of persons, a larger amount of boiling water is used and so a larger amount of heat is thus engendered in the teapot, which has the effect of making the tea taste stronger. Consequently, the rule "a level teaspoon of tea for every cup" may be adjusted if tea is made for a large number of persons.

The other conditions in making tea are:

1. *Teapot.*

Silver or other metal teapots should, if possible, be avoided, and this is essential in making really good China tea, particularly "Cliff tea". Use therefore a porcelain or earthenware teapot. It should be thoroughly rinsed and warmed with boiling water before the tea is put in.

2. *The Kettle.*

Though this is not so important as the teapot, an earthenware one is preferred. In any case, it should be thoroughly rinsed before the water is put in. Any stale water allowed to remain, not to say anything else, would make the tea taste different.

3. *The Water.*

Water to tea, like water to coffee, is a most important element; for, after all, tea is only water flavoured with tea leaves. If the water is not pure or fresh, the tea is more than half spoiled. In China connoisseurs of tea are so particular that they would go for a couple of miles to fetch water from a spring. In any case, if the water is drawn from a tap it should be allowed to run for a while before it is used. Have it boiled to the *bubbling point*, pour it into the teapot, stir it once round with a clean spoon, and let it stand for about three minutes before it is poured out. If any tea leaves are seen floating in the teapot, this means that the water has not really been boiled to the bubbling point.

Any other observations? Yes:

1. Warm the teacup with hot water before the tea is poured in, especially when "Cliff tea" is drunk. The idea is the same as cooling the champagne glass with a piece of ice before the champagne is poured in.

2. Pour the tea into the hot cups half full; for instance, from 1 to 4 (assuming there are only four cups) and the reverse the process by filling them up from 4 to 1, this is to make the tea taste even.

3. Don't continue to pour tea into your guest's cup unless he desires it. Tea not immediately drunk after it has been poured into the cup does not taste good. But don't throw away the tea left in the teapot, if it is China tea; for China tea, after it has been made and kept in a cool place, tastes perfectly good within 12 hours. All to be done is to have it warmed up without the leaves.

4. Keep your tea separately away from other things, because tea is very sensitive in nature and can be easily affected by contact with other things. Very often Chinese travelling to Europe or America have their tea packed in their luggage and afterwards find, to their regret, that the tea is spoiled.

5. Don't keep your tea indefinitely like trea-

sures. The finer the tea, the sooner it should be used and enjoyed. Unlike wine it does not improve with age, except Yunnan tea.

As every feast has its end, so does tea, and so does a book. But a really good meal with delightful company and interesting conversation lingers in one's memory. It is one of those pleasures of life that makes life worth living and inclines one to be at peace with the world. To conclude, according to a high authority, good living is very far from being injurious to health and, all things being equal, *gourmands* live much longer than others.[1]

---

1. *Physiology of Taste,* by Brillat-Savarin, p. 131.